Praise for
Trauma-Informed Yoga

"In *Trauma-Informed Yoga: A Toolbox for Therapists*, Joanne Spence provides an accessible manual of practices that may efficiently restore the nervous system's capacity to regulate mental and physical states. Successful treatment of trauma requires a personal resource to self-regulate one's physiological state and to be accessible to be co-regulated and to co-regulate others. This succinct volume provides an effective and efficient toolbox for therapists working with clients who have survived trauma. It provides detailed instructions for therapists on how to implement specific practices to help their clients regulate their physiological state and to effectively shift from states of threat and defense to states of accessibility and connectedness. The author's own words summarize the power of her contribution: "If trauma is about rupture, then yoga is about connection, integration, and unity." The book reinforces the view that yoga practices provide an important treatment modality for survivors of trauma by providing accessible tools that support well-being and human flourishing."

— **Stephen W. Porges, PhD**, Distinguished University Scientist, Founding Director, Traumatic Stress Research Consortium, Kinsey Institute, Indiana University Bloomington Professor of Psychiatry, University of North Carolina at Chapel Hill

"Joanne Spence has written a magnificent book for mental health care providers, yoga students, and teachers, as well as certified yoga therapists. The book helps us learn how to provide excellent trauma-informed yoga to our clients. Spence offers one of the most clear and concise explanations of polyvagal theory as it applies to yoga and yoga therapy that I have seen in the field. The book finishes with many examples of simple, slow, mini-practices that can be done all day long to soothe and restore our nervous systems. It is clear that she has linked (or yoked) deeply with the topics of trauma, yoga, and what it means to be human. Spence is the author that all of us dream of becoming. She is completely absorbed with the mind of the reader as she writes, which turns out to be a very yogic way of writing. I will definitely use this book in my courses, as it takes difficult concepts and makes them easy to understand for yoga teachers, therapists, mental health care providers, and their clients."

— **Amy Wheeler, PhD**, Professor of Kinesiology at California State University San Bernardino Past president of the International Association of Yoga Therapists

"A must-have for therapists seeking an embodied approach to healing, *Trauma-Informed Yoga: A Toolbox for Therapists* is a wonderfully practical book. Joanne Spence distills her decades of personal practice and yoga teaching experience into deeply informed, yet delightfully clear and accessible, yoga tools. A comprehensive guide, she offers 47 separate practices that you can use with your clients. In part 1, yoga is demystified as Joanne explains how yoga works with the nervous system to help your clients befriend and connect with their bodies to self-regulate. In part 2, she details calming, balancing, and energizing practices designed to prescriptively address your client's in-the-moment needs. Each practice comes with a script and very specific instructions that will empower you as a therapist. *Trauma-informed Yoga: A Toolbox for Therapists* is an essential resource for therapists like me who know that true healing only happens with the body as an integral part of the process."

— **Catherine Cook-Cottone, PhD, RYT**, Professor of Counseling, School and Educational Psychology at the State University of New York at Buffalo and author of four books on mindfulness and embodiment in mental health treatment

"A wonderful, timely toolbox, full of straightforward and practical advice that helps us truly make yoga-based healing accessible to everyone."

— **Christopher Willard, PsyD**, author of *Growing Up Mindful*, Harvard Medical School

"As Stephen Porges, PhD, says, "We are a traumatized species, what does that *give* us?" Fortunately for us, Joanne Spence has done the work in the clinical world working with patients, veterans, prisoners, and school systems to forge tools that leap off the page of her new book and into the body of the reader. Every page left me feeling I was in a nurturing classroom, witnessing mastery as she wisely explored how clinicians can use trauma-informed yoga practices to sensitively build awareness among those struggling with known or unknown traumas. She brings a nobleness to the way she cares for you as the reader and trusts your stewardship of her decades of work."

— **Jill Miller C-IAYT,** author of *The Roll Model: A Step-by-Step Guide to Erase Pain,*
Improve Mobility and Live Better in Your Body

"*Trauma-Informed Yoga: A Toolbox for Therapists* brings out the vast potential of yoga in empowering people to heal themselves. Spence's selection of knowledge-based, skillfully selected yoga practices, as well as her sensitive attention to detail, make this book a must-read for all yoga therapists as they show their clients the path to well-being and wholeness."

— **Shirley Telles, MBBS, PhD,** Director, Patanjali Research Foundation, Haridwar, India
Head, Indian Council of Medical Research, Center for Advanced Research in Yoga & Neurophysiology

"Joanne Spence's *Trauma-Informed Yoga: A Toolbox for Therapists* is a beautifully crafted guide for therapists curious about how to bring the healing benefits of yoga into their clinical work. Using personal stories and trauma-informed tools, she illustrates how to safely explore practices in a slow and gentle way that is deeply respectful of the nervous system. With wisdom gained from her years of experience, Joanne Spence is a trusted guide through principles and practices that honor the needs of the nervous system and lead to embodied well-being"

— **Deb Dana, LCSW,** author of *The Polyvagal Theory in Therapy: Engaging the Rhythm of*
Regulation and *Polyvagal Exercises for Safety* and *Connection: 50 Client-Centered Practices*

"Written with such honesty, love, and holding, the sheer reading of the book felt like a trauma-informed experience. Throughout the text, Spence perfectly captures the ethos of what trauma-informed means and how we as human beings can bring this approach into our entire life, not merely our work. Practical at its core and strongly fortified by science, this book offers a cornucopia of practices that therapists can easily integrate into their work with clients in all stages of their journey while accounting for their unique needs and preferences. Most importantly, she generously offers her own brilliant self-help handouts necessary for clients to cultivate body awareness. I cannot wait to share these with all my graduates and trainees. It was a joyful and vital read. I couldn't recommend it more!"

— **Heather Mason, RYT-500,** Yoga Therapist, MA, MSc
Founder, The Minded Institute, UK

"Joanne Spence has created a guide for integrating trauma-informed yoga into therapy that is equal parts science and heart. Her clear, easy-to-follow instructions make powerful practices seem simple. The warmth she brings to the work helps the reader remember the complex and beautiful humans for which it was created. In every section, Joanne offers inspiration, practical guidance, and reminders of our innate capacity for healing. Thank you, Joanne!"

— **Jennifer Cohen Harper,** MA, E-RYT, RCYT
author of *Thank You Mind: Understanding My Big Feelings on Tricky Days*

"In her new book, *Trauma-Informed Yoga: A Toolbox for Therapists,* Joanne Spence beautifully demonstrates her expertise and experience in counseling and yoga therapy, as well as her deep compassion for adults and youth suffering from trauma, depression, anxiety, and chronic pain. This indispensable guide includes an easy-to-understand translation of the science (finally!), followed by a treasure-trove of simple, accessible yoga-based strategies that are proven effective for supporting client therapy outcomes. Truly, it's a must-have resource for all therapists, and really anyone who seeks to better understand trauma and the mind-body strategies that can assist with healing."

— **Lisa Flynn, E-RYT 500, RCYT,** founder of Yoga 4 Classrooms and author of *Yoga for Children: 200+ Yoga Poses, Breathing Exercises* and
Mediations for Healthier, Happier, More Resilient Children; Yoga for Children-Yoga Cards; and the *Yoga 4 Classrooms Activity Card Deck*

"Joanne's detailed practices are especially useful with veterans who cork compounded trauma in their bodies as though it is the very glue holding them together. The skillfully selected spectrum of practices can help veterans gently peel away the layers of trauma while simultaneously learning to genuinely connect with and care for themselves. The therapists who serve them, who often experience secondary trauma, can also gain self-awareness and embrace better self-care within the therapeutic process. This book will gently help to heal the victims and their healers through self-care, self-awareness, and consistent gentle practice."

— **CPT Jamie D. Sloan, MA, ATR-BC, LPC**, US Army Reserve
Supervisor, Recreational and Creative Arts Therapy Department, VA Pittsburgh Health Care System

"Rediscovering your body after trauma is a central part of healing—and this wise book will help with that process."

— **Johann Hari**, author of two *New York Times* bestsellers, *Lost Connections: Uncovering the Real Causes of Depression*—and the *Unexpected Solutions and Chasing the Scream: The First and Last Days of the War on Drugs*

"Although viewed and often treated as a predominantly psychological condition, trauma and posttraumatic stress disorder have significant physical components and symptoms. This explains why the growing body of research on mind-body practices, such as yoga, is showing significant potential for efficacy for trauma treatment. However, how these practices are applied and instructed is critical to avoid adverse experiences in this very vulnerable population. This book thoroughly covers the basics, as well as the subtleties, of trauma-informed yoga practice and is a valuable resource for trauma patients and yoga practitioners and teachers alike."

— **Sat Bir Singh Khalsa, PhD**, Assistant Professor of Medicine, Harvard Medical School

"I welcome this book! I have had many conversations with social workers and students who wish to incorporate yoga practice into their work. This book not only provides clear instructions as to how to introduce breathing exercises and simple postures, but it also provides evidence as to why yoga works. I will definitely be recommending it to social workers I know and those I teach."

— **Jo Mensinga, PhD, MA, BSW**, lecturer at James Cook University, Cairns, Australia

"This book provides a wonderful organization and clarity to the teaching of trauma-informed yoga. From a theoretical perspective, the principles are laid out in a way that provides a depth of understanding, as well as accessible definitions, practices, and application. Case examples help place the theory in context with practice. Joanne describes and applies polyvagal theory to trauma-informed yoga in a way that encapsulates the lived experience of these states and that allows the reader to walk away with the ability to put these theories into practice. Included are essential practices for categories of calming, balancing, or energizing the nervous system, which help the reader understand yoga through an integrative and non-reductionistic perspective. The practices are provided with clear descriptions, as well as instructions for preparation and ideas for scripts and cueing. These cues connect theory and practice, making them really helpful to the person applying these practices."

— **Marlysa Sullivan, MPT, C-IAYT**, Assistant Professor, Yoga Therapy and Integrative Health, Maryland University of Integrative Health

"The majority of people in this world have experienced some sort of trauma in their lives. Unfortunately, many of us are ill-equipped to deal with these life-altering events. With her new book, Joanne Spence offers the tools necessary to find emotional regulation in our lives. By taking the basic principles of yoga and applying them therapeutically, Joanne teaches us to establish a foundation on which we can build effective yoga practices to self-soothe and focus on the importance of self-care."

— **Giselle Shardlow, MEd,** Founder of Kids Yoga Stories

"*Trauma-Informed Yoga: A Toolbox for Therapists* is full of insightful and informative details. This book has captivated my attention and deepened my appreciation of yoga as an instrument for healing and well-being. It helped me understand the universality of trauma. Joanne skillfully presents research and science that inform the positive outcomes of trauma-informed yoga and make it inspiring. It should be a recommended reading for anyone who works in helping professions and healing ministries, including spiritual directors, spiritual leaders, pastors, and therapists."

— **Rev. Dr. Joan Prentice,** Founder and Executive Director, The Ephesus Project

"Joanne's *Trauma-Informed Yoga: A Toolbox for Therapists* is my new go-to resource. Her sense of compassionate care along with her years of clinical experience make this book rich with knowledge. The practices in the book are adaptable to any age—children, teens, adults, and seniors. With my yoga therapy work in a clinical mental health setting, I am always in search of wisdom and tools that are accessible to all populations. This is a true gift to the growing field of yoga therapy."

— **Ali Popivchak**, Accessible Yoga Instructor, creator of "Yugo, A Yoga Game"

"Joanne Spence has synthesized her decades of clinical service into a resource that is informative and transformational. *Trauma-Informed Yoga: A Toolbox for Therapists* brings a wealth of information, light, life, and humanity for clinicians and those who would like to further deepen their own yoga practice."

— **Phil Mauskapf, MS, MT-BC**

"Joanne Spence has created more than another book about yoga. This book feels like Joanne shares wisdom and decades of dedicated yoga work with the reader with respect and kindness, like having a mentor with you."

— **Aaron K. Teague, MA, MT-BC, LPC**

"Just as we were thinking that we could use an excellent and compassionate yoga therapist for the inpatient acute psychiatric unit at WPIC, Joanne Spence emerged and said yes! She was thoroughly vetted and approved, and she became the first trained yoga therapist to work with patients at WPIC. A pioneer! She not only worked effectively and skillfully but also continued her good work at the hospital for 10 years. Later, her positive energy drew yet another part-time yoga therapist who continued the important work Joanne began. This book will be a valuable resource to practitioners who wish to learn more about yoga therapy and its contribution in mental health."

— **Nancy Rued**, Former Director, Creative & Expressive Arts Therapies Department
Western Psychiatric Institute & Clinic, University of Pittsburgh Medical Center

"Joanne has gifted us with a knowledgeable and practical treasure, a trauma-informed toolkit with easy-to-learn yoga exercises for use by therapists and clients alike. Thank you for providing a bridge to make yoga more accessible to those working with and through trauma. I can't wait to use this resource in my clinical practice!"

— **Mandy Jabbour, LSW**, Living Stones Counseling Services

"A natural educator, Joanne is humble and relatable. She is gifted in connecting with people, in connecting people to themselves, and in connecting people to one another. This kind of genuine connection is inherently healing. I've had the great privilege of attending, hosting, and even assisting Joanne in several trainings though the years. Her gentle, approachable style is unmatched in my experience. I'm so excited to have these practices in a book where I can quite literally hear her voice (Aussie accent and all) as I read her words. The tools in this book will empower clients and be an extraordinary resource for therapists and yoga therapists alike. Like Joanne, I find it essential to use these tools to support my own well-being as I empower and care for others. Kudos, Joanne! Thank you for compiling this valuable resource that will be a go-to for years to come."

— **Polly Manke, E-RYT 500**, Certified Holistic Health Coach,
Holy Fire/Karuna Reiki Master Breathing Meditation Creator and Facilitator

"Joanne continues to dedicate compassion, knowledge, and experience when helping people to help people. This book delivers proven strategies designed to make the life-long process of trauma healing accessible to all. In my opinion as a seasoned yoga teacher, no book of this kind can be helpful without addressing the breath. I'm happy to report that if readers take a deep breath each time Spence references the breath or breathing, they will also experience an extra bonus of clarity and relaxation. Let the healing we can gain from this amazing work begin!"

— **Linda Williams**, Minister and Yoga Teacher, Pittsburgh, Pennsylvania

"Too few resources exist like what Joanne Spence has written here. Those who read it will be learning from one of the best!"

—**Beth Hines**, Chief Program Officer, The Bradley Center, Pittsburgh, Pennsylvania

"This book is a gift, not just to therapists but to anyone who cares for others—clergy, parents, teachers, etc. Joanne Spence has given us a clear, practical, and winsome guide to slowing down and caring for our minds and bodies. Since reading this book, I have begun doing several of these yoga practices every day, have taught some to my daughter, and intend to incorporate them into my teaching."

— **L. Roger Owens**, Associate Professor of Christian Spirituality
and Ministry, Pittsburgh Theological Seminary

"Although the title of Joanne Spence's first book may seem formidable, *Trauma-Informed Yoga: A Toolbox for Therapists* is thoughtful, highly readable, and reflective of her abiding passion for teaching. Having participated in one of Joanne's sessions with a group of students from Saudi Arabia, I now have an even deeper appreciation for her teaching methods and her genuine desire to help people become more aware of their bodies. If this first book is any indication, Joanne's readers have much to expect from her in the future!"

— **Gail Shrott**, Executive Director, GlobalPittsburgh

"This is an accessible and user-friendly guide to understanding complex scientific theory and to feeling confident to lead others in simple yoga practices. As a yoga educator who works primarily in the high school setting, I have seen firsthand how timely the arrival of this book is. Our young people were already reporting alarming levels of depression and anxiety even before the collective trauma of the pandemic began. This book can help with the collective trauma affecting young people, educators, families, and society at large."

— **Iona M. Smith, MEd, CYT 500**,
Program Leader for Kripalu Yoga in Schools and a RISE™ facilitator

"Whether you are healing from your own trauma, work with trauma survivors, or love a survivor, this book is for you! This gentle, insightful, and deeply informed resource will add many well-honed tools to your own toolbox. *Trauma-Informed Yoga: A Toolbox for Therapists* makes healing possible!"

— **Robin Capcara, MA**, Campus Minister and Spiritual Director
Carnegie Mellon University, University of Pittsburgh, Duquesne University

"Joanne's book is life-changing for those of us working with trauma survivors and for those who support them. There is so much out there about mindfulness, yoga, and trauma-informed practice, but Joanne's book brings it all together and teaches us how to scaffold our learning. Joanne has succeeded in breaking down polyvagal theory and making it more accessible. I feel like I understand so much more now about how to integrate the theory in order to practically and therapeutically support people who have experienced trauma. We have known for a long time that "the body remembers," and to thrive, survivors need more than talk therapy. This book takes us through many practical exercises to help the body and, in doing so, to help the individual thrive. Importantly, I also understand why I need to be "firmly anchored in a ventral vagal state" myself as I prepare for all my work with other human beings. The reality of "co-regulation in action" deeply resonates with me. Joanne's book is just what I need to better manage my own health, as well as better support others."

— **Kandie Allen-Kelly, BSW, MPhil**, Registered Accredited member of the Australian Association of Social Workers,
Graduate of the Australian Institute of Company Directors, and Professional Mediator Member of the Resolution Institute

"Joanne Spence has created an invaluable resource for therapists to integrate healing, stabilizing yoga practices into mental health settings. Her teachings are both precise and elegant. Of note, Spence has a gifted ability to communicate the complexities of trauma-informed yoga in a wholly practical way. The format of this book allows therapists with different levels of yoga experience to access foundational knowledge and practices as needed. This book will no doubt be a source of mind-body integration for many therapists and their clients."

— **Abby Wills, MA**, Movement, Mindfulness + Social Emotional Development
Specialist at Full Circle Consulting Systems and Co-Founder of Shanti Generation

"I am very grateful for Joanne Spence's book, *Trauma-Informed Yoga: A Toolbox for Therapists*, which is a helpful blend of the neuroscience that undergirds the practice of yoga, the basic framework for initiating an intentional yoga practice, and numerous detailed practice suggestions. As a school counselor, I have already taught some of her practices to students in kindergarten through the 10th grade, with great reception. In this period of record levels of anxiety among school-aged children, Joanne's book is right on time. Helping young people become emotionally regulated through the body, so they can engage with their whole selves in their whole life, is our goal as counselors. I am grateful this book provides us with the framework and tools to help them along the way."

— **Karen F. Boyer, MSW, LCSW**, School Counselor, The Ellis School

"Joanne Spence makes a valuable contribution to the ever-expanding field of trauma-informed yoga and its application in the traditional field of psychotherapy. As a psychotherapist myself for almost 20 years, I regularly teach my clients many of the simple, yet effective, exercises Joanne presents in this book. My heart fills with compassion as I imagine the countless individuals who will benefit from Joanne's offering."

— **Dana Moore, MAR, MA, LPCC**, Kripalu Yoga Teacher, O.S.B. Oblate

"Joanne is an expert in her field who has constructed an invaluable toolbox for therapists. Her experience and love for her work is felt throughout the pages, and the tools presented are essential for those who wish to deliver trauma-informed practices."

— **Andres Anirt Gonzalez**, MBA Co-founder, Holistic Life Foundation, Baltimore, MD

"This is such a timely book when the trauma of the pandemic and political strife—as well as being Zoom-weary—continue to take a toll on our physical and emotional well-being. While this book is intended for therapists, the way Joanne has written it makes it a wonderfully accessible toolbox for a much wider audience, including (but not limited to) spiritual directors, classroom teachers, and medical professionals—essentially anyone wanting healthy, uncomplicated practices for coping with stress and trauma. I will unequivocally be drawing on it for my spiritual formation courses. And, on a personal level, the simplicity and variety of the breathing exercises Joanne offers has enriched my embodied prayer life immensely. This is a book I will return to over and over again!"

— **Dr. Leslie F. Thyberg, PhD**, Learning Skills Coordinator, Adjunct Pastoral Theology, Trinity School for Ministry

"As Joanne Spence lays out the foundations in the first four chapters of her book—providing clear definitions of various terms, describing the foundational principles of yoga, articulating the basics of trauma-informed yoga, and giving a very clear and easy-to-understand overview of polyvagal theory—a number of things become clear: Spence's deep care and concern for her reader, and for her students in general, come through vividly. She wants them to always remember the importance of self-care and, at the same time, to be fully informed regarding the theoretical foundations of trauma-informed yoga.

The final five chapters contain 47 different calming, balancing, and energizing practices—and here again, Spence's care for the needs of her readers, and the special care with which she provides numerous tips for her fellow teachers, is striking.

The book is easy to read and comforting in that you feel like you have a good friend supporting you all the way through, encouraging you to explore these wonderful practices and to discover, as she did, their powerful potential to bring about a deeper sense of connection and mind-body-world integration."

—**Don Salmon, PhD**, Clinical Psychologist and Co-creator of https://www.remembertobe.life/12-week-e-course

"This book is a must-read for practitioners helping those suffering from trauma. Another tool to help your patients and yourself."

— **Dr. Cynthia Zurchin**, CEO Positive Consulting, Retired School District Superintendent

"Joanne Spence confronts the harsh reality of trauma with a powerful, yet gentle and body-based, method of healing. All trauma, whether overtly physical or invisibly psychological, takes place in the body where our wounds are stored, waiting to be seen. It makes complete sense, then, that healing cannot be completed without the participation of our bodies. As a trauma survivor myself, and a body worker who has worked solely with survivors, I know firsthand the healing that is possible through breath and movement. I highly recommend Spence's book to therapists of all backgrounds."

— **Carmen Berry, MSW**, *New York Times* bestselling author,
CEO of Berry Powell Press

"In this accessibly written book, Joanne Spence draws upon polyvagal theory to present the neurological basis as to why yoga practices that integrate body, mind, and breath offer a way to augment trauma-informed care. Through Spence's warm, gentle style of teaching and leading of specific yoga practices, I have witnessed how these "tools" can calm, energize, or balance the energy of participants during intensive training workshops and enhance their readiness to learn. As a psychologist, spiritual director, and supervisor, I use these yoga practices to enhance not only my work with clients but also for my own self-care. This book will lead you step by step to incorporate these practices in trauma-informed care in your own field of work."

— **Martha A. Robbins, ThD**, Founder and Director, Pneuma Institute, Licensed Psychologist, Spiritual Director, Joan Marshall Associate Professor Emerita of Pastoral Care, Pittsburgh Theological Seminary

"Joanne Spence has written a gem. Weaving together theory, practice, and anecdote (as well as a good helping of winsome humor!), she has created an accessible field guide for caregivers that explores the intimate connection between the body and mind in recovering from trauma. By grounding her work in a practice we all share—breathing—Spence gently reminds us of our shared humanity and the agency we all possess to participate in our own well-being. Our bodies hold knowledge just as surely as our minds do, and the integration of these ways of knowing is crucial to the work of healing. And given the pervasiveness of trauma in our communities, we are all but guaranteed its presence in our clients and loved ones, whether disclosed or not. Simply put, if you are in the business of caregiving, this modest book with its equally unassuming practices has the capacity to transform your work and will become a part of your toolkit that is essential as, well, breathing."

— **Helen Blier, PhD**, Director, Continuing Education, Pittsburgh Theological Seminary

"*Trauma-informed Yoga: A Toolbox for Therapists* is a timely work of practical scholarship. The traumatic impact of a pandemic afflicted world has presented itself in need of what Spence offers, especially for frontline healthcare workers suffering from spiritual and moral distress and who may find traditional spirituality and religious practices an insufficient balm for their entropic condition.

— **Rev. John C. Welch, M.Div., PhD** is a medical ethicist serving on the ethics committees of two major healthcare systems in Pittsburgh, Pennsylvania.

Joanne's work is a robust resource for everyone supporting those affected by trauma and moving toward healing, resilience, and growth. Her approach is accessible, practical, and inspiring, not only in its depth of knowledge but in the overwhelming spirit of connection and support that shines through on every page."

—**Amy Secrist, MA**, Certified Yoga Teacher, Certified Mindfulness Based Emotional Resilience Yoga (EMBER) Teacher, Certified Mindfulness Educator

TRAUMA-INFORMED YOGA

A Toolbox For Therapists

47 Simple Practices to Calm, Balance,
and Restore the Nervous System

Joanne Spence, MA, E-RYT 500, C-IAYT
Foreword by Amy Weintraub

Published by
PESI Publishing
3839 White Ave
Eau Claire, WI 54703

Cover: Amy Rubenzer
Editing: Jenessa Jackson, PhD
Layout: Bookmasters & Amy Rubenzer

ISBN: 9781683733461

Printed in the United States of America.

PESI Publishing
pesipublishing.com

About the Author

Joanne Spence, MA, E-RYT 500, C-IAYT, is a recovering social worker and certified yoga therapist. She has a Social Work degree from James Cook University and a Master of Arts from Pittsburgh Theological Seminary. She is the founder and executive director of Yoga in Schools.

Joanne trains and teaches all sorts of amazing people, both nationally and internationally, in yoga. She has taught yoga in prisons, hospitals, schools, churches, and sometimes on street corners. She specializes in working with adults and children who are experiencing chronic pain, trauma, depression, anxiety, ADHD, and insomnia.

Joanne draws on more than thirty-five years of clinical experience as a mental health professional and twenty years as a teacher and practitioner of yoga, including ten years as the first yoga therapist at Western Psychiatric Institute and Clinic. She is in private practice as a yoga therapist and a spiritual director at Urban Oasis Pittsburgh and works with veterans on several behavioral health units in Pittsburgh teaching therapeutic chair yoga. In addition, Joanne leads in-person and online trainings on yoga, mental health, trauma, and contemplative practices.

Joanne has co-authored several published articles as well as a chapter in *Stories of School Yoga: Narratives from the Field,* and she was a contributor to *Best Practices for Yoga in Schools.* Joanne likes nothing more than to demonstrate the inclusive nature of yoga practice; if you can breathe, you can do yoga.

Joanne has been married to Doug for over thirty years. Together, they have three adult children, all of whom practice yoga! When she is not teaching, Joanne loves to read, write, hike, travel, cook, and even dance a little—just not all at the same time.

Visit her website at joannespence.com.

Dedication

In loving memory of Christina Carlucci Wilson (1961–2019) and Elizabeth Ann Marshall (1968–2019), two of the best "sister" friends a girl could have. I loved and admired you both deeply, and I believe the feeling was mutual. I miss you daily. Christina and Beth, this book is for you and your dearly beloveds: Jim, Benn, Emily, and Sam—and Allan, Doug, and D'Arcy, respectively. When times were rough during this project, I thought of you and knew you would want me to finish well. So I did. I will never forget the friendships we have shared.

Table of Contents

List of Practices

Foreword

By Amy Weintraub

Joanne Spence's *Trauma-Informed Yoga: A Toolbox for Therapists* comes at a time when trauma is impacting our lives in a variety of ways. Children are growing up in an era of increased school shootings, seventy-seven percent of whom will develop post-traumatic stress disorder. Many are also the witness or victim to sexual and physical violence. Similarly, seven out of every ten adults in this country have lived through a traumatic event at least once in their lives. This means that someone sitting in your treatment room who presents with a relationship issue—or, if you happen to be a yoga therapist, a bad back—might also be a trauma survivor who will benefit from a trauma-informed approach to treatment. It means that when you are facilitating a treatment group or leading a yoga class, a number of your clients might numb out, disassociate, or collapse because you say something simple like, "You are safe here" or "Try holding your breath." Someone with a history of trauma may be feeling fine in the session until the word *safe* reminds them of their core belief: There is no safe place in the world. Their earlier experience is the proof, and you've just reminded them of that. Similarly, someone who was smothered during a sexual attack might freeze when asked to *hold their breath*.

What is beautiful about trauma-informed yoga as described by Spence is that it gently begins to peel back the defensive layers that may have been essential for surviving the trauma but are now no longer necessary. By attuning to their breath and body sensations, clients create a window of presence that allows them to regulate their nervous system and move into a place of balance. The body is always present. The mind is a time traveler. The practices that Spence outlines here, such as gentle breathing practices, or slow and accessible movements in a chair, invite clients and students into a felt state of presence, allowing a temporary pause in the stories they may be telling themselves about not being safe, good enough, or lovable. As Spence suggests, engaging in these repeated practices can gradually open the window of safety in the present moment until we and our clients are living with more ease and less reactivity.

Spence makes everything accessible. Her language is clear and, because she's been there and is honest about her own journey, she understands the challenges of beginning something new and then teaching it to others. In one of the clearest explanations of Stephen Porges's polyvagal theory that I've ever come across, Spence shares her forays into workshops and trainings to better understand this game-changing theory. She describes the same eye-glazed, overwhelmed feeling I've experienced when lectures become too scientific or unrelated to what would best serve my yoga therapy clients. It is from this perspective that she breaks down the information in a manner that even I can understand. And you will too.

This is not a yoga book that adheres to a lineage or even a particular school of yoga. Spence is careful to honor the source of the practices she offers—recognizing that they are grounded in ancient traditions, most of which originate from India—but she adapts them for use in clinical settings. Because of her experience in teaching in psychiatric settings, her work with various trauma populations, and her special training in LifeForce Yoga and other trauma-informed modalities, you can be confident in Spence as a guide.

I encourage you to try these practices for yourself to see how you feel. If you aren't doing much in the way of breathing practices or daily meditation for self-care, even one five-minute practice Spence suggests can make a difference in your life. You may already be a yoga practitioner and know what I mean. The increased peace and clarity you feel after a short practice can also affect your therapeutic work. For example, what if you led that same five-minute practice in a session with a client who has a history of trauma and who arrives in your office with racing thoughts and speech? What if, as Spence suggests, you began the session with a simple ritual, like lighting a candle, taking a few guided moments of silence, or practicing the breathing practices in this book? Do you think that would help foster your therapeutic alliance? After many years of training therapists in the LifeForce Yoga protocols, some of which are adapted in this book, I can answer with a resounding yes. And as research has shown, one of the best predictors of successful treatment outcomes is the therapeutic relationship. As you try on and co-create practices with your clients, you empower them to be an active participant in their healing and, as Spence suggests, give them agency over their lives. As you practice together, not only will those you serve feel calmer, but you will too.

You may wish to seek further training in the practice and application of yoga, but this book is all you need to start. It will help you (and your clients) boost your mood and experience days that are defined by ease, no matter the long list of to-dos.

Amy Weintraub, MFA, E-RYT 500, YACEP, C-IAYT, is the founder of LifeForce Yoga and a pioneer in the field of yoga and mental health.

Acknowledgments

I have been dreaming of this moment for a very long time. I wrote this book in a relatively short amount of time: nine months. But the reality is that it has been writing itself for the last twenty years or so. As with many authors before me, I was somewhat surprised at how many people it takes to write a book when writing itself is such a solitary practice. As the mother of three adult children, I liken the process to the lifelong commitment of parenting; it takes a great community of people.

It is a challenge to think of how to thank *everyone*. First and foremost, I am grateful for the leadership and mentoring of Amy Weintraub, who has so eloquently described my intentions for this book in the foreword. You are a great example of living what you teach. Some folks have *felt* most every step of this process and have lived it with me. Some of you have been there for me with your time, expertise, creativity, and (sometimes) a cup of tea when I emailed, called, or turned up at your doorstep even if you didn't know me (yet).

Of the many people I wish to acknowledge, I would like to begin with Nancy Rued and Jamie Sloan - gritty women in leadership—who have created a path for my teaching in environments that have mountainous bureaucracies. I also wish to thank Heather Mason, Catherine Cook-Cottone, Deb Dana, Melanie Burns, and Jane Ellen Stevens. Thank you to Stephen Porges for returning my emails, answering my questions, and taking the time to edit my chapter on polyvagal theory. In addition, I want to thank: Marlysa Sullivan, Rose Kress, Iona Smith, Alan and Linda Komm, Tanya Sullivan, Lisa Flynn, John Stahl-Wert, Andrea Hyde, Sat Bir Khalsa, Louise Goldberg, Jen McCaslin, Mary Shan Overton, Donna Giver Johnston, Renee Prymus, Katrina Woodworth, Stephanie Bell, Kelly McLellan, Amy Secrist, Kelsey Reagan, Tish Harrison Warren, Mari Stout, my prayer supporters through my faith community and the Pneuma Institute, and the faculty, staff, and students of Pittsburgh Theological Seminary.

Also special to me are my yoga teachers over the years: My first yoga teacher, Beth Shaw, the late Bekir Algan, Leah Kalish, Susi Hately, Jill Miller, Sarah Court, and Kristine Kaoverii Weber. And, of course, my students at Fitness Yoga, Yoga on the Square, and Urban Oasis Pittsburgh.

Thank you as well to my therapist friends and colleagues who have been willing to allow me to "test" my practices: Beth, Ali, Rachel, and Paula.

I am so deeply grateful to Karsyn Morse and the whole team at PESI, for taking a chance on a first-time author, and for Jennifer Cohen Harper (Founder and CEO of Little Flower Yoga) for introducing us. Jenn, you are my hero. I also couldn't have asked for a better editor than Jenessa Jackson. It felt humbling to know that someone was giving such careful attention to the words I had labored over. I felt seen, heard, and respected. I struggled to bring some of my ideas and knowledge to life in a coherent fashion. You have made me look good!

If there were medals to give, surely Leslie Wright would receive one. When I owned various yoga studios, Leslie taught yoga with me and was a former high school English teacher. At some point in this project, she offered me the gift of her undivided attention on a weekly basis. It was a long, slow, arduous process. In addition to grammar, you helped me flesh out my ideas more fully. And, at times, we laughed until we cried when you would bring to my attention a practice that I had written that was actually impossible to execute—which of course was not my intention. You can thank Leslie for that, indeed, you do not need to be a pretzel to do the practices. She would wisely say (after wiping her tears), "I don't think that is what you meant to say." She never failed to cheer me on. I may never understand *parallel structure or dangling participles*, so if I got it right, it's thanks to her and my editors. If not, the errors are my own. I owe you big time, my friend.

To my friends and family in Australia and in England: Thank you for checking in and for your interest, whether or not you understood what I was up to. I can't wait to give you books in person as the year unfolds. Mum, thanks for always believing in me. It means a lot.

My children, Merryn, Jacob, and Lucca, have been true champions of my work and encouraged me every step of the way. It means so much to be able to leave this legacy of work for you. Each of you have been an integral part of my yoga journey. From inspiring me to want to get well after the car accident that changed everything; to working the front desk at our yoga studios, sweeping the floor, and putting props away; to eventually learning to be yoga teachers yourselves and joining me at workshops and conferences as my colleagues. A mama couldn't be prouder of the awe-inspiring people you have become. But just in case you've ever wondered what I have been up to while you were at school, this book will fill in those gaps for you.

Lastly, everyone needs a first reader. Mine is my best friend and husband, Doug. This doesn't work in some marriages. At times, it has been tricky for us to navigate the different roles. There have been some wild highs and lows. But after thirty-four years of marriage, we seem to have found our way together. I could not be more grateful for your love and support of my crazy aspirations.

Introduction

This book is a how-to manual for two types of therapists: **(1)** those who are not familiar with any type of yoga practice or its utility in talk therapy, and **(2)** those who have heard about the marvels of yoga and mindfulness but have not found an accessible way to bring such practices into day-to-day therapy without investing lots of time and money. With this book, you can learn how and why to incorporate elementary, yet effective, aspects of gentle movement and breathing practices into your work. These practices are grounded within a basic understanding of how trauma affects the nervous system so you do not unintentionally recreate trauma for a client disguised in the form of treatment.

As I was putting the finishing touches on this book, I had nearly an hour-long video chat with a young Israeli combat veteran—the wonders of technology! During our call, he told me the story of his mandatory time in the Israeli Defense Force and how this experience had negatively impacted his life. After being released from the army at age twenty-one, he didn't seek help for ten years, after which he finally "woke up" and finally reached out for help. He soon realized that other young combat veterans had similar struggles and eventually formed an organization to allow them to process their experiences peer to peer. Now my young friend spends his time giving lectures and talks on university campuses. His organization has a presence on eleven different campuses in Israel and operates through individuals called *ambassadors*.

We talked about the need for accessible tools that people of any age and ability can use to cope with depression. He is a yoga teacher himself and often teaches people alternate nostril breathing, but he wondered if I had any other practices that could help. I told him I did and, right then and there, over video chat, we engaged in the practice of stairstep breathing. He said the practice made him feel tingly and awake. He felt it in his chest. We agreed to stay in touch. These are fairly common occurrences for me: meeting someone who would not ordinarily have anything in common with me, yet we find common ground through the simple, essential act of breathing. No matter your tribe, country of origin, or social status, trauma is no respecter of persons.

Although you might not be seeing combat veterans in your practice, it is very likely that you will see people who have overwhelmed their capacity to cope with the day-to-day ups and downs of life that could well be related to past trauma. And it is possible they may not have the words to tell you what is going on. That's where this book can help. This book provides you—the busy and conscientious practitioner—with yoga-related tools and practices you can use as an adjunct to talk therapy.

Although I have deep respect for talk therapy and consider it an essential part of my own healing journey, it has its limitations. If you are reading this book, then I am assuming you, too, are looking for new ways to connect with your clients. Perhaps you could benefit from a practice that will move therapy forward or are simply looking for ways to assist clients in connecting viscerally to their body. Or perhaps you've noticed your own attention wandering in session. Is there some occasional boredom, frustration, or malaise on your part? Do you feel talked out? If so, then trying some of these yoga practices may be life-changing for you and your clients.

My own personal experience of trying yoga was one of desperation rather than curiosity. I had been in chronic pain for two years after a car accident, and as the saying goes, I was sick and tired of being sick and tired. And I was open to the possibility of being well again—even if it meant having to try something called yoga. I was working at a health club as a water aerobics instructor, and when the club offered to train existing instructors in yoga, I thought, "Why not?" Besides, the club was paying for the course.

That first weekend of yoga was filled with anxiety, pain, and self-doubt. I realized I was in over my head and thought I should probably quit while I was ahead. First, all the other trainees taking the course seemed to know something about yoga. Second, they looked fit and bendy. I had been working hard in physical therapy but could barely get out of bed in the morning. I wondered how something that looked like stretching could be so hard and boring. Although I made it through the end of the weekend, I came away chagrined. My instructor kindly pointed out that I just needed to practice (no kidding!), and she added something that has stayed with me: *Because you are coming from a place of injury and illness, you will have more compassion for people in your classes who are just like you.* Over time, these words proved to be true. But the dramatic turn happened three days after my initial yoga encounter. I was pain-free for the first time in two years. I woke up and felt like I got my life back. It took me a few days to recognize the link between doing yoga and being pain-free, and when I did, there was no turning back.

When I finally started teaching therapeutic groups, many people had already decided that they were "not the yoga type" or "not flexible enough" to participate—particularly if the word *yoga* was in any way associated with it. This sentiment became so common that I wondered if we should avoid the word altogether. Certainly, yoga has been co-opted by so many that the ancient sages might not recognize what passes for yoga today in the West. In fact, I once invited a thirty-something male veteran to a therapeutic chair yoga class and his response was, "Yoga? What's yoga? Yoga is pants—you know, yoga pants. Yoga is not a class." He was serious. So what exactly *is* yoga?

The word *yoga* itself means *union.* I see yoga as an integration of the body, mind, and breath. It involves a rich and deep tradition of informing how we live in our body and the importance of harnessing the lifeforce we call breath. Breathing is good news because you are doing it already. Automatically and without conscious effort. And that's where this book comes in. This book will draw from a large body of knowledge to present you with a modest, yet solid, repertoire of effective movements, postures, and breathing practices that lend themselves well to the counseling office or small group practice. I am going to help you build on what you know and do.

WHAT THIS BOOK IS AND IS NOT

This book is a practical approach to offering simple mind-body practices to your toolbox. Specifically, this book will arm you with knowledge (the why) and with powerful, yet simple, activities that reduce suffering and increase well-being (the how). This book is not a comprehensive tome on yoga practice or the eight limbs of yoga. It cannot be that. Nor is it meant to be an academic paper on the highlighted practices. Reading, digesting, and practicing the tools in this book will not make you a yoga teacher or an expert in yoga practice. Nor will it make you a trauma therapist.

However, this book will give you a solid, introductory understanding of (1) the prevalence of trauma and why the particular practices affect the nervous system, (2) how to implement these practices into your own work, and (3) how to teach them to others in a clinical setting. You will also learn how our emotions are affected by our movement and breath, and why we need to actively seek ways to stimulate our parasympathetic nervous system on a daily basis. Whether you are a seasoned practitioner looking to supply yourself with new tools or are at the beginning of your career, the practices in this book are straightforward and readily accessible so you can help your clients get out of their head and into their body.

If the tools highlighted in this book become a useful and enjoyable part of your practice—as I hope they will—then I encourage you to seek additional in-person training. I have included some suggestions in the resource section of this book. However, if even a handful of the tools humbly offered here become your go-to yoga practice, then I will consider the time it took to write this book worthwhile.

WHAT TO EXPECT

This book is divided into two parts. **Part 1** includes philosophical and background information that will help ground your practice. Here you will find fundamental concepts and definitions, a description of the foundational principles of yoga, and neuroscience research highlighting the relevance of the polyvagal theory in working with trauma. The information in these chapters will provide you with the rationale for incorporating gentle movement and breathing into your sessions.

Part 2 provides you with the actual practices. The practices are divided into four categories—calming practices, balancing practices, energizing practices, and visualizations and meditations—so you can better understand how they differ from each other, although in many instances you will find that they overlap. The description of each practice will reveal why it is important, when to incorporate it in session, and what to expect from the practice. There will be ideas for how to transition them into your sessions.

Most of the tools and exercises described in part 2 can be performed while sitting in a chair. The dosage—or the amount needed to feel an effect—is surprisingly small. In order to stay within the scope of your practice, please don't exceed the maximum dosages suggested here. I assure you that more is *not* better and, in fact, could be counterproductive.

HOW TO USE THIS BOOK

Ideally, I suggest you read the book from beginning to end so you can get answers to any what, when, why, and how questions you may have. But you can also go straight to the practices and decide which tools you believe will be most helpful. Do what fits your learning style and needs. Be intentional about including these tools and practices in your sessions. Commit to your practice and then, well... practice! While the experience of trauma is complex, practicing the trauma-informed tools in this book is not. By including gentle, slow, and rhythmic movement linked to breath, real changes can occur in our emotions and our bodies.

So what's the catch? The catch is that you must *do* these practices for yourself *first*. Do not simply give your clients a homework handout and say "Try these." The practices work best when you do them with your clients—or alongside them. When you know in your body that they work, you can preach what you have been practicing. Therefore, you need to put this book down at some point and try some of the exercises because reading about them only goes so far. Knowing skills, theories, and interventions is not the same as doing them. How often do we read books or take courses on some topic that has piqued our interest, only to have the lovely spiral-bound course handout gather dust on our overstuffed bookshelf? The actual *doing* is key.

If certain practices seem too simplistic to have any real value or to result in lasting change, please look again and try them for yourself, much like you would try on an outfit before buying it. See if it fits. Although yoga is not a stand-alone medicine or panacea for all ailments, it certainly is worth a second or even third look as a credible and valuable addition to any treatment plan. I am still surprised at the power of these practices even after practicing and teaching them for so many years. May it be the same for you.

In addition, if you ever find that very slow movement is lame (a non-technical word I hear a lot!) or that simply noticing your breath is a waste of time, I would say two things. First, a heartfelt thank you for being honest. I felt the same way for a long time (longer than I care to admit). Second, you are not alone in your thinking. Convincing people that slow is good can be a hard sell. And to be frank, it can seem boring or even unsexy at times. While this may be true, it isn't a reason to not practice and teach these tools. In fact, it may be in those slow, boring moments that you find some peace and quiet from an overly stimulated or anxious mind.

This book exists as an antidote to living life in the fast lane. Surprisingly, small doses of movement and attention to the breath can create significant changes in our functional movement patterns and in our nervous system's ability to regulate itself. This work is empowering and very good news for anybody who has struggled with depression or anxiety, or anyone who is just plain *stuck* in some way. In addition, it can be good news for any clinicians who have been diligently practicing their profession only to discover they have symptoms similar to their clients (Reuben, 2015).

My hope is that these practices will become part of your repertoire of tools to care for yourself. In doing so, I hope you have a long and satisfying career while avoiding burnout, secondary trauma, and cynicism. At the same time, I hope you experience the satisfaction of seeing your clients become *unstuck* and move forward in their healing journey.

PART ONE

The Philosophical and Practical Why

CHAPTER 1

DEFINITIONS AND BACKGROUND

TRAUMA

According to the American Psychological Association (2020), trauma is an emotional response to a stressful or distressing event, after which individuals commonly experience shock and denial. They may also experience "unpredictable emotions, flashbacks, strained relationships and even physical symptoms like headaches or nausea. While these feelings are *normal*, some people have difficulty moving on with their lives" (American Psychological Association, 2020, emphasis added). Trauma can also occur when someone witnesses a distressing event or is indirectly exposed to it, as is often the case for first responders, humanitarian workers, and even bystanders.

Trauma is not rare, as we once believed. Nor is it confined to combat violence or major disasters. In fact, it's estimated that ninety percent of individuals seeking mental health services have been exposed to some form of trauma, with many experiencing multiple traumas, prompting some to view it as an epidemic (Huckshorn, 2004; Kilpatrick et al., 2013). For the purpose of this book, I use the term *trauma* in its broadest definition as *anything* that happens to us that overwhelms our current ability to cope. This means trauma isn't something that only happens to some people—it is all of us: family, friends, neighbors, and co-workers. In other words, trauma affects all of us in some way.

Because of the prevalence of trauma, it is likely that you or your client have experienced trauma of some kind, though not everyone who experiences trauma needs treatment. When we assume that we all have some sort of trauma in our lives, the information can be contextualized when formulating a treatment plan that promotes healing and growth.

TRAUMA-INFORMED

Trauma-informed "anything" has become a buzz phrase in health care and other related fields. There are now whole movements that rally around being trauma-informed, from trauma-informed health care to trauma-informed communities, to trauma-informed schools and trauma-informed correctional facilities, to name just a few. The first time I heard the term *trauma-informed* was in 2008, when I was at a mandatory training at Western Psychiatric Institute and Clinic. At the time, the term was associated with an emerging realization that some forms of mental health treatment were retraumatizing already traumatized patients. In turn, a trauma-informed approach was being developed to address trauma in the lives of children and adults without retriggering the original trauma. This approach was a response to the groundbreaking Adverse Childhood Experiences (ACE) study, which found staggering correlations between childhood trauma and negative physical and mental health outcomes later in life (Felitti et al., 1998).

As I was doing research for this book, I was deeply moved by the story that led to the ACE study. Dr. Felitti, a preventative medicine specialist, had been doing research for years on weight loss and obesity. Over time, he became increasingly puzzled about why his most successful patients would relapse. He was determined to find out the cause, which led to multiple interviews, mostly with women from his research studies. Eventually, he found a common denominator. He discovered, almost by accident, that each person had been sexually abused right before they gained significant weight. He also discovered that the women saw the weight gain as a protective mechanism that made them "invisible" and therefore safe from further abuse. One woman who had been sexually assaulted told him, "Overweight is overlooked, and that's how I need to be" (Felitti, 2002, p. 44). Thinking this finding would be headline news, at least among his peers, he presented his findings at a national conference on obesity. But his findings were not met with the excitement he expected. Instead, the response was lukewarm at best, and dismissed at worst, and he realized he needed to do more. This meant forging partnerships (Hari, 2018).

That's where things got interesting. Dr. Felitti was introduced to Dr. Robert Anda, a medical epidemiologist with the Centers for Disease Control (CDC). This powerful partnership was what Dr. Felitti needed in order to make his point. Between 1995 and 1997, they surveyed over 17,000 patients of Kaiser Permanente's Medical Care Program, who were subsequently followed for an additional fifteen years. Neither of them could have predicted the extent of how significant the data would be. They found that adverse childhood experiences (termed "ACEs") predicted a wide range of negative health and social outcomes in adulthood, including heart disease, diabetes, alcoholism, and cancer. In addition, patients who reported one ACE were likely to experience multiple ACEs—and those with multiple ACEs were at increased risk of these negative health outcomes. Only about one third of participants reported having no ACEs at all.

Since the ACE study was first published in 1998, over seventy scientific articles have been published, and scores of conference presentations have been delivered. Other researchers have referenced their work more than 1,500 times. Today, there are national conferences and websites (such as www.acestoohigh.com) that provide connection, education, and services to people with ACEs. A simple Google search of "ACE Study" results in over 300,000,000 possibilities. However, the ACE study has yet to have the sort of policy effect and behavioral change one would hope for. Think of the societal changes that happened after the 1964 Surgeon General's Report on Smoking and Health. Over the following decades, the number of smokers fell dramatically. What will it take for us to see a similar dramatic decline in ACEs?

Despite the wide-reaching impacts of the ACE study, I am always surprised at the high number of people in the mental health field who are not familiar with the study or who have not heard of the term *trauma-informed*. This has steeled my resolve to write this book – to give you accessible trauma-informed tools that you can incorporate into your work. These tools are effective and safe, even if your clients don't present with a trauma history. As a clinical psychologist and colleague pointed out to me, there are many reasons why someone may show up in your office or treatment facility, and it may only be a matter of time before you unearth something unexpected. When this occurs, having a toolbox of trauma-informed practices will be of immense benefit to you and your client. I am advocating that *all* your work be trauma-informed, regardless of whether you call yourself a trauma therapist or specialist or have additional training in treating patients with trauma.

The importance of being trauma-informed and maintaining an awareness of ACEs is well illustrated by the story of Anna Jennings, who died by suicide at age thirty-two while in a California state treatment hospital, where she'd been receiving treatment for seventeen years—eleven of which were as an inpatient. The tragedy of Anna Jennings's death is a disturbing example of someone who was retraumatized by treatment that only served to compound her suffering. Her mother, a mental health advocate and Maine's first director of the Office of Trauma Services, pointed out in hindsight Anna's high ACE score. No one had ever performed a trauma assessment on Anna, despite Anna's own revelations to her treatment providers about her illness and traumatic past (Jennings, 2007).

It is important to note that using the word *trauma-informed* does not involve defining people by their trauma. We are all more than the trauma that has occurred in our lives. Rather, it involves acknowledging one's trauma history in the service of promoting healing and growth. It is a person-centered, healing-focused approach to treatment that takes into account the neurological, biological, and social effects of trauma. According to Dr. Gordon Hodas (2006), trauma-informed care has many facets:

> *It refers to recognition of the pervasiveness of trauma and a commitment to identify and address it early, whenever possible. Trauma-informed care also involves seeking to understand the connection between presenting symptoms and behaviors and the individual's past trauma history. As a practice and set of interventions, trauma-informed care involves professional relationships and interventions that take into account the individual's trauma history as part of efforts to promote healing and growth. (pp. 5–6)*

According to the Substance Abuse and Mental Health Services Administration (SAMHSA, 2014), there is a six-step approach to being trauma-informed: (1) safety, (2) trustworthiness and transparency, (3) peer support, (4) collaboration and mutuality, (5) empowerment and choice, and (6) cultural, historical, and gender issues. These steps are intentionally broad and general because being trauma-informed is not about a checklist or an approach per se. Rather, being trauma-informed "requires constant attention, caring awareness, sensitivity, and possibly cultural change" at multiple levels and constant checking for quality improvement (CDC, 2018). This is true whether you work in private practice, a hospital, a government-run agency, or a not-for-profit organization. Being trauma-informed requires your constant attention.

In addition, there is an important distinction between trauma-informed care and trauma-informed treatment:

> *The latter involves specialized treatments that some individuals also may need to address complex trauma-related consequences. Trauma-informed care, in contrast, is not highly specialized and can be provided in multiple settings by committed professionals who understand trauma without the expertise to offer trauma-specific treatment, which can be offered as needed by designated staff or through referral. (Hodas, 2006, p. 6)*

This distinction is important in clinical practice. For example, even if you are not a specialized trauma therapist, given the prevalence of trauma, you most likely will work with clients who have experienced trauma—whether or not they disclose their trauma history or are even aware of it themselves.

Therefore, we must institute some *universal* precautions, or *best* practices, when it comes to trauma. Think of the handwashing campaigns of the previous decades that were instituted to reduce the spread of infection and are still reinforced today. We now know much more about infection control than we did in previous generations, and still, the number one recommended action to reduce the spread of disease is handwashing. It is a simple thing to do, anyone that has access to clean water can do it, and in certain settings, it is a requirement. Just like handwashing is the best way to prevent infection, a universal approach to trauma-informed care is an idea whose time has come. Soon, this approach will become common, and it will gradually become easier to be trauma-informed and to offer trauma-informed practices. You will start seeing things with new eyes.

TRAUMA-INFORMED YOGA

There is overlap between how the phrase *trauma-informed* came to describe health care and how it is used to describe a particular way of teaching yoga. But they are not the same thing. I first learned about trauma-informed yoga during a week-long training with the LifeForce Yoga Healing Institute in 2009. The institute trains yoga and mental health professionals in the use of clinically appropriate yoga practices that support those with anxiety, depression, and post-traumatic stress disorder (PTSD). In this professional setting, I learned that while yoga provides many benefits that contribute to our physical and mental health, it can also trigger or exacerbate existing mental health problems. For example, problems can arise when yoga teachers give hands-on adjustments without asking permission first or when they insist that a student execute a pose in a very specific way (failing to recognize that all bodies are different). Or problems can result from the physical postures themselves or by a lack of focus on the breath when transitioning between poses. This is not an exhaustive list of potential problems, but it represents a good starting point.

When I first began taking yoga classes, I myself had visceral reactions in my own body that I did not understand. It became clear to me that this practice—one that I know and love and that had helped heal my own body, physically and mentally—was also a potential minefield to someone with trauma. Therefore, at that juncture in my teaching career, I committed to making sure that all my teaching was trauma-informed, whether I was teaching in a yoga studio, a psychiatric hospital, or anywhere else. The efficacy of gentle, slow yoga was too valuable to allow it to be diminished by *not* making trauma-informed teaching my universal practice.

Most of the time, even in hospital settings, I do not know the medical or trauma history of the people in front of me. Complicating matters further is the realization that not everyone who has a trauma history *knows* they have a trauma history. A yoga class may well be the place where a person first gets an inkling of such knowledge. These realities highlight the importance of establishing trauma-informed yoga as a universal practice, much like handwashing in health care is a universal practice.

Trauma-informed yoga is not a treatment. Rather, it is an understanding of trauma, its prevalence, and how to generally accommodate people (in yoga classes) who have experienced some sort of trauma. Trauma-informed yoga offers a lens of support that makes space for any potential ways someone could feel or respond to triggers, trying to prevent re-traumatization in every way possible.

The primary themes in trauma-informed yoga include open and invitational use of language that creates a safe and welcoming space, clear boundaries, no physical touch unless clearly consensual, a normalization of symptoms or responses to movement, and grounding, centering, and breathing techniques that lead to self-regulation (Khouri, 2019).

Although trauma-sensitive yoga has also been coined as a training approach for individuals who have been through trauma, it is not the same. Trauma-sensitive yoga represents a specific and intensive adjunct *treatment* for trauma survivors (David & Hopper, 2011). While there are some overlaps between the two, trauma-sensitive yoga focuses on treating individuals who have been diagnosed with PTSD, which is different from being simply trauma-informed.

In chapter 3, I will provide some additional information regarding yoga, including the steps needed to deliver the practices in this book in a trauma-informed manner. Additionally, the appendix includes twelve trauma-informed principles for growth (Cook-Cottone et al., 2017) as a resource for yoga teachers.

YOGA

It is beyond the scope of this book to fully describe what yoga is. Tomes have been dedicated to doing just that. However, Dr. Catherine Cook-Cottone (2015) provides a helpful definition in her book, *Mindfulness and Yoga for Self-Regulation*:

> *Yoga is defined as a mind/body practice comprised of physical postures (asanas), breath work, meditation, and relaxation. Through the teaching and practice of yoga, yoga teachers facilitate an experience of positive embodiment that promotes mindful awareness, self-regulation, and physical fitness. (p. 283)*

The practice of yoga is designed to unify many things. For the purpose of this book, I use the word in a most basic way: to unite the mind and body with the breath as Cook-Cottone states. I sometimes get asked why I call the practices in this book *yoga* when perhaps *mindful movement*, *mindfulness practices*, or *somatic practice* might do the job just as well. That may be true, but all the practices in this book, whether or not they actually arise from a lineage of yoga, I have learned from twenty years of participating in yoga classes or trainings.

The yoga presented in this book is secular in nature, meaning that it is not tied to any religious practice. In addition, when I reference yoga throughout this book, I am referring to modern yoga and the evolution of yoga taught in the West. At the same time, it is important to acknowledge the roots of the practice of yoga, which originated in India over 5,000 years ago. Although a full discussion of this topic is also beyond the scope of this book, some yoga scholars have suggested that what is taught in the West today is a blend of yoga and European calisthenics, some of which has little resemblance to the earliest teachings of classical yoga in India (Singleton, 2010, 2011). While I agree with this perspective, honoring and learning about yoga's cultural and historical roots is a rich and fruitful pursuit, albeit for another book.

At the time I opened my first studio in 2003, I probably knew about thirty yoga postures and a handful of breathing practices. That was it. However, I have always thought it important to teach what I know, which wasn't much at the time, but it allowed me to gain experience and to eventually grow my knowledge base. Today, I teach far fewer postures—focusing mostly on those that are accessible from a chair—and many more breathing practices. But what my teaching has always been about is self-care and self-awareness for all body types and abilities. In fact, if I had to describe yoga in just two words, I would choose *self-care* and *self-awareness*. That's it in a nutshell for me. Of course, it is true that yoga is more than this, but if the importance of self-care and self-awareness is all you take from this book, then I have met my objective.

Referrals

If you want to refer clients to a yoga class or a particular yoga teacher, it is important that you understand that simply telling your client to go take a yoga class may not be helpful. Rather, a clinician's decision to recommend yoga should be treated with the same care and professionalism as any other type of referral. Do some homework, try some classes, and reach out to yoga teachers in the community to find out if any share your philosophies. Ask folks in your network if they take yoga and, if so, find out what they like about the class or the teacher. Is the class slow and gentle? Is it advertised as a trauma-informed or trauma-sensitive class? Does the teacher have an understanding of trauma or have specialized training? Generally speaking, look for classes that have the words gentle or restorative in the title. Or a class that emphasizes breathing practice. Building relationships with yoga teachers who are knowledgeable on such matters will make your job easier.

GENTLE MOVEMENT

I do mean gentle, as in slow. Really slow. So slow that you may be tempted to nod off. In fact, whenever I teach a chair class in the afternoon, I usually tell my students that nodding off is common and that they shouldn't feel embarrassed if this happens. (However, if I nod off while teaching, that can be problematic!) Why so gentle? It's not because I think that's all you can muster but because learning how to move slowly and gently is an intentional practice. It is hard to move slowly. Of course, we can't move at this sort of slow pace all the time or we would never make it to breakfast! But in practicing slow and gentle movements, we learn how to express compassion toward ourselves. We seek to nourish and honor our own well-being. Being gentle with ourselves helps this type of self-care to happen. Rather than trying harder, try softer (Kolber, 2020).

As Timothy McCall explains, "Yoga is strong medicine but it is slow medicine" (2017, p. 8). However, today's fast-paced culture doesn't always look favorably on slow or gentle. People want what they want, and they want it *now*. And we have all heard the "no pain, no gain" mantra of the fitness world. If that's you, then I want you to ask yourself if that is truly working for you. I know there was a time in my life when I would always choose a movement class with "boot camp" in the title over anything that said "slow" or "gentle." *But I didn't know what I didn't know.* My hope is that as you and your body get more acclimated to slow and gentle movements, you will actually begin to crave them. In paying more attention to the mind and body, you will start to *hear* the messages that your body is sending you. And when you listen to the body's whispers, you don't have to hear it scream (Hately, 2010).

BREATHING EXERCISES

The one thing we all have in common as a species is that we breathe. We don't even have to think about it. It just happens automatically. As simple as breathing is, it is far more than sucking in oxygen and expelling carbon dioxide. Yogis call the breath our *lifeforce* or *pranayama* and believe that the control of the breath is the key to robust physical and mental health. In their book, *Breathe In, Breathe Out*, Drs. Loehr and Migdow talk about the power of the breath as follows:

> *Research has shown that slowing down and deepening our breath shifts us from the stress response to the relaxation response; this slows the heart, normalizes blood pressure, increases blood flow to the digestive system, deepens sleep, increases energy, focus, concentration, and memory—optimal breathing not only helps prevent or cure disease, it raises performance levels in school and sports. (1999, p. 3)*

With benefits like these, who needs a marketing department? Science now supports what has been known, intuited, and felt for generations—if not millennia—via the practice of breathing awareness during yoga. In fact, we now know that breathing practices can shift the body's autonomic nervous system out of a state of fight, flight, or freeze and into a state of calm by activating the vagus nerve. In chapter 4, I'll go into more detail about the nervous system and the mechanism of breathing as an agent of change.

All the breathing exercises in this book are informed or inspired by my substantial yoga training. I did not make them up, though I have modified some practices for use with individuals who have no yoga background whatsoever. I have used these breathing exercises across a range of settings, including in my private practice, in public classes, and at various psychiatric institutions, and I have found that anyone can benefit from these simple, yet effective, practices. In fact, I think breathing practices are some of the most surprisingly powerful—and most underutilized—tools on the planet.

Cindy's Story: The Power of the Breath

In the mid-2000s, I met Cindy Zurchin, a principal on special assignment at a school where I was offering after-school yoga programming. Cindy had been assigned to the school because of its high proportion of children with behavioral issues. Any time I entered the school, the environment had a palpable chaotic and frenetic energy about it. But when I began introducing yoga to the children, Cindy saw for herself how well they responded to the program. And like many teachers, she was amazed that a social worker (me)—not a classroom teacher—could actually handle and **teach a** roomful of dysregulated children. I'd like to say it was because of my stellar teaching techniques, but it wasn't. Up until that point in my social work career, I'd mostly worked with clients one-on-one and in small groups. In becoming a yoga teacher, I'd somehow overlooked the fact that I had little experience working with groups of children. So whatever miracles Cindy saw, it was the power of the practices themselves—*not* my teaching prowess. In my experience, when you create the right conditions, the most unlikely of folks want to learn to relax their bodies and feel peaceful.

Cindy realized the teachers needed these resources for their own well-being, and under her guidance, she gathered the other school leaders and a handful of teachers to figure out a yoga path for the whole school. Cindy's enthusiasm and leadership led the way. She understood the mind-body connection and championed the cause of body movement and connection to the breath. Through it all, her advice to other teachers and counselors was this: Begin where there is interest, and build from there. Respect people's differences, and then give them simple resources. *Catch them doing good*, and affirm the small changes and attempts they make. Though it was not Cindy's job to work one-on-one with students, overwhelmed teachers often would bring students to her office. Of Cindy's many stories, this one sticks out:

There was a little guy who was moving around from school to school. The records that followed him were full of behavior issues. Everything from not listening to assaulting other students. As I started to talk with the young man, he was "very pumped up." I asked him to just sit back in his chair with both feet on the floor and to close his eyes. He immediately said, "What are you going to do to me?" I told him we were going to breathe together. "Let's breathe in through our nose and fill up our belly. Try to hold it for a few seconds, and then blow it out through your nose." We did this together a few times, and I noticed he had relaxed his entire body and had a smile on his face. He asked if we could do it again.

A few weeks later after working informally with him, he told me, "Calming yourself down is not that easy." We later discovered he was very bright, yet other schools thought he should be tested for special education programming. The student had an older brother who was incarcerated and had witnessed more in his short life than most people do in a lifetime. When he learned to manage his emotions and the school staff supported him, he was able to excel academically.

MIND-BODY CONNECTION

Most of us are familiar with the term *mind-body connection.* This could just as easily be called (and sometimes is) the body-mind connection because the terms refer to a two-way street that works in both directions. Most of us are familiar with how the mind affects the body. For example, when we are watching a movie, we might laugh, cry, or fear for the characters on the screen. We know the characters are not real, but the emotions we feel as we watch their drama unfold certainly are real. We feel the emotions in our bodies as we notice ourselves tearing up or our muscles tensing, even though we know full well that what we are watching is not reality. But, let's face it, sometimes it feels good to engage in drama that is not our own. The engagement of watching someone else's drama can connect us to our emotions and be cathartic.

At the same time, just as our mind affects our body, what we do with our bodies can shift our mood. The more we understand and practice this simple phenomenon, the better we become at repeating it when we need it the most. For example, think of how good it feels to stand up, take a deep breath, and stretch your arms overhead when you have been sitting at your computer for an extended period of time. The mind is able to take a break, which is triggered by the movement of the body. It is a win-win situation.

Even individuals who are confined to a wheelchair have some control over how and when they move their body. This control is the very nature of *personal agency*, which is the ability to control certain aspects of our lives. Life has a way of showing us that there are things we have control over and other things that we do not. For instance, it is easy to agree that we have no control over the weather. I also had no control (or input) as to whom my parents would be or that I would be born in the U.K. and immigrated to Australia when I was three. However, when I met my future husband at an aerobics class, accepted his proposal of marriage (not at the aerobics class, but six weeks later...), and immigrated to the United States, I *chose* to do so. I had agency.

Why am I spelling out the concept of agency so clearly? **Because learning to practice yoga can facilitate personal agency as individuals come to learn that they have a choice in deciding how to move their body. This choice gives them some sense of control over their lives.** During my ten-year period working in an inpatient facility, many of my clients felt as if they had no control over any part of their lives. This impotence did not actually exist, but that's how it felt to them. My role as a yoga therapist was not to confirm or deny their present reality—whatever that was—but to help them notice that, even in a locked psychiatric facility, there were things they had control over, even if that was deciding whether or not to participate in my yoga class. The act of noticing opened the door to exploring what else they might have control over. In this way, they could have agency in their life.

The simplicity of this starting point should not be underestimated. Personal agency is the common denominator that we all can relate to, whether we are in an acute care psychiatric setting or struggling to get through our workday. And by making the willful choice to move our body and connect to our breath in some way, we can tether ourselves to the present moment. The body and the breath are always in the present, unlike the mind that likes to time travel to the past and to the future. Yoga can teach us a great deal about how we might move and use the breath to anchor ourselves to the present and connect to our body.

This action of connecting to our body is extremely important because we are more than the sum of our thoughts and emotions. The body has its own intelligence. The practices in this book will help your client connect to their body, and it will also describe the benefits of doing so. These benefits are achieved by regularly engaging in practices that foster self-awareness. **Noticing or being aware of what is happening in our bodies in the present moment is a skill we can cultivate and nurture until it becomes second nature.** Although much has been said about present-moment experience, this book aims to break down preconceived notions about what this term means by getting to the nitty gritty of actual practice.

CHAPTER 2

FOUNDATIONAL PRINCIPLES

In this chapter, you will find ten foundational principles that are essential for understanding how and why the recommended practices in this book work. I have incorporated these foundational principles into every practice described in this book, whether directly or indirectly. These ten teaching points emerged as I reflected on what I teach the most, the words I use to describe my teachings, and my many years of observing the effect of my teaching to those in front of me. When describing these foundational principles, I use various key phrases when teaching and leading *all* the practices. My use of these particular phrases accomplishes two things: It demystifies the practices by using common, jargon-free language, and it provides repetition, which is helpful for learning and recall. Phrases like "activating the sixth chakra" may be perfectly suitable and appropriate language in a yoga workshop but not necessarily in a therapy session. I find that keeping my language simple, clear, and concise clarifies the experience and makes it more accessible.

While there are ten foundational principles, I use two every time I teach any of the practices in this book: (1) linking breath to movement and (2) moving only in a pain-free range of motion. Your clients will become familiar with these key phrases, and this process will provide you and your client with a common language. As you read through the foundational principles and experience them in your practice, perhaps different words will emerge for you. What matters is that the knowledge base you develop translates into action by those you are teaching. It is repetitive action (practice) that leads to skills.

There is nothing proprietary about these foundational principles, as they are common to many practices that enhance well-being. They are not new or original. These principles are distilled from twenty years of teaching in many different settings, hundreds of hours of training, feedback from students and clients, and my own journey of healing. I have chosen these ten principles based on actual feedback from students and clients regarding what was most effective for them.

My best teachers have always been my students and clients, and they will be yours too. I always ask for feedback, either verbally or nonverbally, so I can reflect on what I am doing and how I am doing it. Gathering written feedback may be as simple as giving people index cards and asking them to write down three things about the session that surprised them. This encourages people to dig deeper into their own learning process and yields useful data for both of you. Gathering verbal feedback can be as simple as asking, "How is this landing with you right now?" or "What are you noticing about nasal breathing?" If a client hesitates, I may demonstrate a thumbs up or thumbs down sign to encourage them to share. I want to be sure to give clients permission to not like a particular practice, as this often gives me as much information as when they do like a practice. Make it easy for people to share their insights with you. Carve out a few minutes. Keep it simple.

Creating the space and guiding people as they connect with their bodies and emotions can be a very tender and beautiful thing. When I guide large groups, I can feel the energy of the group shift.

For example, I recently began to lead a group of forty male veterans, mostly in wheelchairs, whom the program director had described as rowdy. But now when I arrive, they quiet themselves and are *ready* to do chair yoga. Often, staff will hug me afterward or mention how it's their favorite day to come to work because they get to practice with the veterans and feel a sense of peace after. The staff often remark how surprised they are to see the veterans engaged in chair yoga. I see it too but am not surprised. The potency of the practices is often underestimated. Don't let yourself become jaded or too self-conscious to try them. Embrace the opportunity, whether it's your first time or you already engage in some of these practices and simply needed to be reminded of their benefit.

1. LINK BREATH AND MOVEMENT

Linking breath and movement may seem like a foreign concept at first, but this is what distinguishes yoga from other types of movement. We intentionally link the breath with movement and notice what happens. At first, you will need to repeatedly remind yourself (and your client) to link breath to movement. But over time, you will notice that you begin to do so even when you are not practicing. Or at a minimum, you will start to notice when you are breathing and when you tend to hold your breath. It is very helpful to begin noticing this pattern in yourself.

With each exercise, we are trying to cultivate ease. Why? An important concept in yoga comes from Pantanjali's Yoga Sutra 2.46: *sthira-sukham asanam* (Satchidananda, 1985). It is commonly translated as cultivating ease and steadiness in each pose or being comfortable and finding stability in each pose. We can only cultivate this ease and steadiness if we are breathing slowly and smoothly.

Linking breath to movement is a key first step to developing awareness. It is a huge thing for a person to realize that there are specific movements and thoughts that cause them to hold their breath. I see it regularly in the veterans I teach. Many want to do some yoga but think it is impossible since they are physically or mentally compromised in some significant way. Perhaps they are in a wheelchair or have had a limb amputated. Or perhaps they are having suicidal thoughts. Practicing linking one's breath to movement can be a helpful guide to regaining one's equanimity. As we slow the breath, we activate the calming part of our nervous system called the parasympathetic nervous system. The actual mechanics of how breathing activates this part of the nervous system are discussed in chapter 4.

The act of noticing that you are, indeed, breathing is the starting point for linking breath to movement. The next step is noticing *how* you are breathing. Is it a long breath or a short breath? A smooth breath or a ragged breath? Are you breathing through your nose or mouth? Once you have this level of awareness, it becomes easier to make some simple changes to how you are breathing. I am often asked if there is a right way and a wrong way to breathe. The answer is *it depends on what you are doing*. For example, it is not wrong to breathe through your mouth, particularly if you are congested and if this is the only way you can breathe. Doing the best you can should be your default mode.

At the same time, the science of breathing can inform our knowledge base as to why we might want to switch to nasal breathing if this is not our default method of breathing. For example, nasal breathing helps release oxygen from the blood, allowing it to circulate to our tissues and organs (McKeown, 2015). Our nasal hairs also warm, filter, and humidify the air we breathe in. Nasal breathing engages the diaphragm and is silent and almost invisible; it is light and soft. I describe the practice of nasal breathing in part 2 of this book, and I recommend you put in some time to get really good at it. While that may sound silly, nasal breathing can take practice if you are not doing it most of the time. To begin, simply close your mouth and breathe in and out through your nose. Although there is more to it than that, it's a good place to start.

Scott's Shortcut to Nasal Breathing with Children

I remember first meeting Scott Mandarino early in my yoga career. He was an energetic and dedicated elementary health and physical education (HPE) teacher at an inner-city pubic school (and still is, at the time of this writing). He had many children in his classes who struggled with emotion regulation and impulse control. He had his hands full. One day he saw me teaching yoga in the hallway and was surprised, to say the least, but also puzzled. "Why aren't you in the gym?" he asked. Good question. This occurred before programs like Yoga in Schools was a *thing*. Eventually, though, I began teaching in the gym with the support and enthusiasm of teachers like Scott.

The plan was for me and other Yoga in Schools staff to teach a portion of Scott's HPE classes while he apprenticed as a yoga teacher. After one *fairly* hectic third grade class that seemed more or less successful—no one got hurt, and the kids were on an even keel when they left for their next class—Scott smiled and said, "I've never seen that before." He was referring to the instruction I had given the children: Put your top lip on your bottom lip. When the class followed my instruction, there was no talking, and they had to breathe through their noses. It had worked! Fifteen years and hundreds of kids later, Scott still uses this cue with kids. "It sure beats telling them to sit down and be quiet!" And I still use it too, even with adults.

2. ONLY MOVE IN YOUR PAIN-FREE RANGE OF MOTION

During an almost ten-year stint of working several days a week as a yoga therapist at Western Psychiatric Institute and Clinic, I was always amazed at how many people presented with physical pain in addition to psychological pain. The physical pain was often a barrier to their desire to participate in a yoga group, even if it was chair yoga, and it forced me to think carefully about how I could support my clients to move, even a little bit.

The phrase "only move in your pain-free range of motion" became my rally cry. It may sound like a bit of a mouthful, but it needs to roll off your tongue often and easily. I will often mention my own experience of coming into the practice of yoga following a serious car accident and let clients know that my ability to move changes each day as a function of my activity levels, the season, the quality of my sleep, and so on. I often demonstrate a very small amount of movement and then progress to a larger amount depending on how my body is doing that day. Many people need the visual demonstration and permission to do less movement rather than more, along with the verbal instruction, to be able and willing to find their pain-free range of motion. I usually will be very emphatic and say, "I mean this literally. Although I am not a mind reader, I can often tell if you are overdoing it because I tend to overdo things myself, and I know what to look for. I will let you know if I think you may be overdoing it. However, with practice, you will be able to monitor yourself."

We all know what it is like to overdo things and regret the result later. For example, I often overdo it by lifting something that is too heavy for my frame to move easily. When I see people overdoing it in a group, rather than calling them out individually, I may simply repeat, "We are moving only in our pain-free range of motion" and "Less is more." I will also remind clients to notice their breath, "Your breath will guide you. If you are holding your breath, you are doing too much. Let your breath guide you." I let people know that I will be saying this phrase again and again. I don't think you can say it too much. You may feel self-conscious at first, but the hope is that clients will eventually do this for themselves. And they do.

If you work with people who have chronic pain, you may be considering whether to refer your client to physical therapy. And perhaps you should. However, I have seen many clients who have maxed out their physical therapy benefits (if they had them in the first place) and who are depressed as a result of long-term pain. This was my own experience. Two years following my accident, I was still in pain—everywhere and nowhere in particular. It was confounding to me and my doctor. It gave me a glimpse of the thin line between pain and depression. I often see people who have tried *everything* and no longer know where to turn for help. They hear things like "I have nothing else to offer you" or "I can find nothing wrong with you." Daily life becomes an unending struggle, and that's when I get the call: "I am desperate enough to try yoga."

Helena's Story of Chronic Pain

Helena came to see me at the recommendation of a mutual friend who knew of my work with chronic pain. She fit the category of "I am desperate enough to try yoga." Helena had been experiencing pain for three years due to chronic sciatica. She had tried physical therapy, traction, chiropractic care, and cortisone shots, but to no avail. She finally considered surgery when a pain specialist told her that she risked permanent nerve damage if the cause of the sciatica wasn't fixed. An orthopedic surgeon assured her that the surgery wasn't a big deal and that she'd be "good as new" within six months.

Following surgery, Helena was anything but good as new. Once an avid traveler, she barely felt well enough to go to her sedentary job. She was unable to walk or stand for more than a few minutes at a time. Over time, her depression worsened, and she felt very isolated, unable to make even small trips from the house. Her situation finally came to a head when, after a year of struggle, her orthopedic surgeon told her there was nothing more he could do for her.

When Helena walked (very slowly) through my door, I felt quite daunted by her story. I knew yoga had helped me and so many others, but where to start? I didn't want to hype my ability to help her heal or promise something that yoga could not deliver. However, I did want her to have hope, so we agreed on a "let's try some things and see how it goes for a few months" plan.

We began with the most fundamental principle: the breath. She started to notice and pay attention to her breathing as she practiced the foundational principles in this book, gradually incorporating them into her day. The breathing and key poses came easily to her, particularly when she could do them in a chair. In addition, she focused on maintaining daily routines centered around sleeping, eating, and hydrating. Little by little, Helena began to feel stronger and more in control of her life. We then worked on increasing her walking time—only moving in her pain-free range of motion—and gradually her functional movement and mood improved. Eventually, she was ready for us to walk half a mile to her favorite coffee shop and have a victory lunch.

The big breakthrough came when she booked a flight to Europe, followed by a week-long tour of a city she had yearned to visit for many years. In her darkest days of pain, she had ditched the idea of ever leaving the country again. But she did it. Now she is trying to decide where to go next. Her journey wasn't easy, and there were plenty of barriers, but she kept practicing and working on her daily routines. Her advice to you is this: Be patient, especially as you develop new habits. Accept the bad days without blaming yourself. And don't give up.

The practices in this book will help strengthen your client's capacity for functional movement and build a sense of ease in the body that has been missing because of pain or fear of pain. Don't be afraid to start with simple breathing practices. People in chronic pain do a lot of breath-holding just to get through the day. If you can simply get them to pay attention to their breath and to find even a tiny bit of ease, some tension in their body will dissipate. As with most of these foundational principles, it's easier said than done. We often overdo it and tell ourselves that a small amount of movement isn't worth the effort. *But it is worth the effort.* Being able to move, even in a small way, is essential to regaining a fuller range of motion. Even imagining movement (when movement is not possible) can benefit our body and brain (Mulder et al., 2004).

Ultimately, pain is an important signal to the body that tells us all is not well. It is an output of the brain designed to protect us (Moseley, 2011). We need pain to show us our limits. Feeling pain and learning to move in a pain-free way is essential to functional movement. These two things may sound paradoxical, but they can coexist. Moving in a pain-free range of motion does not mean that the physical pain does not exist. But to find it requires slow, thoughtful movement linked to your breath.

3. MAKE FRIENDS WITH YOUR BODY

Making friends with your body is exactly what it sounds like. Instead of being at war with your body—either by overindulging or ignoring it—befriend it. This can be difficult for clients who have experienced an illness, an injury, or some type of chronic pain because they no longer trust the body to do its job in signaling what is safe, life sustaining, or threatening. This often results in a sense of being betrayed by the body. Making friends with your body means rebuilding trust, as you would in any relationship. The idea of treating and cultivating one's body as a friend and not an enemy can be tricky to navigate but well worth the investment of time and compassion.

So how does one go about making friends with the body—and through yoga in particular? The notion of dialectics, which is central to dialectical behavioral therapy, can help. Dialectics involves holding two seemingly opposing ideas as true at the same time. One common dialectic is the notion of acceptance and change. We can *accept* ourselves as we are while also acknowledging the need to *change*. Instead of berating ourselves when we get things wrong or make a mistake, radical acceptance involves acknowledging that mistakes are bound to happen because we are human.

This type of radical self-acceptance is a necessary component of befriending one's body. Everything about each practice—the gestures, the tone of voice, the slowness—needs to communicate kindness and compassion toward ourselves. We meet ourselves wherever we are in that movement, honoring our self and asking what our body might need in that moment. In yoga, this is consistent with the ethical principles of *ahimsa*, which means non-harming. We can cultivate *ahimsa* by befriending ourselves; being kind to ourselves both physically and emotionally.

We can start with our own words and gestures, only speaking to ourselves like we would to a loved one. This quiet, contemplative practice of being with oneself and speaking kindly to oneself—either inwardly or out loud—is usually the hardest part for many of my clients. They may stumble over words or get stuck with no words. Often there are tears. For clients with chronic pain, you may need to make room for feelings of sadness or grief that come with the sense that their bodies have betrayed them.

I always say things such as, "Thank yourself for caring for you today. You did this yoga practice for you. I was just the guide. It was your effort and participation that made the practice what it is for you." No matter how good I may be as a teacher, I can't *make* people do things (I've tried!), and neither can you. I think it is very important to continually point out that clients are doing the practice of their own accord. They are *choosing* to do it (for whatever reason). This choice gives people a sense of personal agency. Consent is powerful. While all the practices in this book are designed to cultivate a loving relationship with the body, if this principle in particular is calling you, try *hand on heart, hand on belly* (chapter 9, practice 2).

Several of the practices use affirmations written in simple, strong, and loving language. Some of my critics have wondered how I can get away with saying such "cheesy" things (their word, not mine), especially when working with a group of war-ravaged veterans or suicidal teens. Observers are amazed and sometimes skeptical. I have a few responses. First of all, I am not sure what *cheesy* means. One guess is that means "overly sentimental." But what I think my critics are asking is why these loving affirmations are necessary. Doesn't everyone know their own worth as a human being? In actuality, many people *don't* love themselves, and even if they do, the self-affirmation bears repeating.

Second, if you can't authentically say loving things about yourself and to yourself, then don't attempt to do so with another person until you can. Having grown up in Australia, I have noticed a sarcasm in American culture and speech that is often lost on me. It is worth examining your own cultural bias and noticing what assumptions you may bring to the counseling space. If you can't practice self-love and radical acceptance, it's okay to save the practice for another day. Finally, if *cheesy* means cliché, when did loving and caring for yourself become a cliché? And besides, I like cheese.

4. SLOW DOWN

During my thirteen years as a yoga studio director in Pittsburgh's east end, my colleagues and I often hosted weekend workshops for yoga teachers. After one workshop, one teacher quipped, "I never knew slowing down could be so exhausting!" as we stumbled slowly to our cars, wondering if this newly relaxed state left us fit to drive home. Her comment is characteristic of many I hear from students and clients after a therapeutic yoga class. *Yoga is surprisingly exhausting.* Well, not exactly. Yoga can release or settle any pent-up tension and busy thoughts, which allows us to recognize when we are exhausted or sleep deficient. It helps our body recognize these very important signals and respond to them with messages of kindness and care, such as taking a nap or doing less.

Moving slowly is hard. There is nothing easy about slowing all our movements and breathing patterns. It takes time and practice to move slowly in an intentional way. For me, slow movement was a hard-fought battle. Why walk when running or jogging could get me there faster? Although I am still a fan of speed and efficiency, something deep inside me has changed. Now, I can move slowly at will. As silly as it sounds, it took me many years to master the art of slowing down. It did not come easily or naturally to me. If I slowed down too much or was still for too long, I would fall asleep. When I share this experience with others, it surprises people who assume I have always talked softly and slowly and enjoyed restorative yoga. I am simply proof that, over time, practice can help rewire one's nervous system and change one's behavior.

Today, the art of slowing down applies to more than my movement and breathing. I also relish slow, unhurried chunks of time in my day. A great day for me is an unhurried one in which I am able to do one thing at a time instead of rushing from one thing to the next. This unhurriedness is a huge change—even a confession—for someone who prided herself on her ability to multitask. But now, an unhurried day has breathing room, perhaps some silence, and reflection time built into it. It feels wonderful. And it is the opposite of what I thought for a very long time was a good day.

My youngest son, Lucca, was a major instrument in teaching me to slow down my day. He was two when I opened my first yoga studio, and he got used to being patient and flexible with his serial entrepreneur mommy. But I clearly remember the day when we got in the car to run various errands and he innocently asked, "How many things are we doing today, Mommy?" I didn't know. I was thinking, *Until my whole list gets done, Bud.* Without too much thought, I replied, "Three things. We are doing three things today."

A little later, after the third stop, we got back in the car and he said, "We're going home now, right? You said three things." Well, I wasn't nearly done with my list. I realized I had been a little ambitious with my answer and wanted to advocate for more time. Then I remembered that I was the adult in charge and that words are important. I took another look at my list and stole a glance at my new accountability partner, who was barely three feet tall, and I answered, "Yes sir, home we go." I was rewarded with a big smile and a high five. Sometimes our best teachers come in small packages. That day, I learned that we can practice letting go of our need to do so many things in one day, and the world goes on anyway.

When we slow down, it creates a buffer between us and the rest of the world. There is more room to experience life as it unfolds in front of us. For example, if I am rushing around from activity to activity without any margin for error, I tend to get upset if there is traffic, a road closure, or heaven forbid a passerby or neighbor who wants to chat before I speed away. While I'm not saying that I always need to make small talk with strangers or chitchat with my neighbors, I do value being hospitable and welcoming as one of my core values. But I can't honor this core value if I am always rushing from one place to another in the name of getting more done. I miss the opportunity to encounter ordinary, everyday things right in front of me.

When we move at a slower pace, we can more clearly notice our surroundings, as well as the sensations and feelings going on in our bodies. This allows our body's innate intelligence to guide us into pain-free functional movement and to stop us before we injure ourselves. But we have to be listening. At the same time, I recognize that people often use fast movement as a coping strategy, and I'm not going to take away someone's coping strategy if they are not ready to "try on" slow. For example, I have had veterans tell me that when they slow down, all the physical and mental pain comes rushing into their mind and body. When clients rely on fast movement as a coping mechanism but also desire to move at a different pace, I recommend trying one small change at a time. They can do something as simple as slowly driving (observing the speed limit) to do their next errand. Or they can take a slower pace to walk their dog (if they have one). I ask clients to notice how this slower experience felt. It is not wrong to move through the world quickly, there are just other ways to do so.

So the next time you are tempted to rush through your day, remember to slow down and breathe. Know your limits. Find some ease. Be present and open to what is right in front of you. You will still get things done. But don't take my word for it, experiment for a day and see what happens.

5. PRACTICE SELF-CARE

Some people think *self-care* means being selfish, but nothing could be further from the truth. As an adult, it is your job to care for yourself and to own your own stuff—the whole package. No one else is lining up for the job because it's your responsibility. Therefore, practice self-care like your life depends on it—because it does. I was hoping to avoid using the airplane safety metaphor here, but it effectively communicates the message we all need to hear. You've probably heard it quite a bit if you have flown anywhere: In the event that the cabin loses pressure and the oxygen masks drop from overheard, put on your mask first before helping your child or other people around you. Why? Because you can't help anyone if your brain is oxygen-deprived and you pass out. The same principle applies to the practice of self-care. You need to take care of yourself first before you can take care of, assist, and serve others (even your own children).

So what comes under the rubric of self-care? Does it mean going to a day spa or getting a massage? Well, on a really good day or for your birthday, maybe it does! But self-care can be much simpler than that. At its core, it is about knowing yourself and listening to what your body needs. It may be as simple as remembering to drink enough water, going to the bathroom when you need to, eating lunch on time without a screen in front of you, or jealously guarding your night-time sleep schedule. (There's a checklist in the appendix if that would be helpful.) It can also involve knowing when to call it a day, instead of continuing to push yourself, and getting the rest you need.

The goal of self-care is to make it a part of your lifestyle—and not just an add-in when you can. It is something to integrate into your life without guilt or apology. For example, my husband, Doug, often falls into the gender stereotype of not going to the doctor unless death seems imminent. Not long ago, he finally decided to act on a long-standing health issue. I watched his progress from being challenged by something he read, to calling his doctor to make a plan, to finally implementing the plan. I was thrilled and amazed. I realized that doing a cheerleading dance—as entertaining as that might be—might border on sarcasm and be patronizing, so instead I quietly told him that I wanted to thank him for something I noticed him doing. I reiterated the message, "You cared for yourself in a very tangible way"—which he has heard before (ad nauseum)—and that both of our lives were richer for him taking his self-care seriously.

6. DEVELOP SELF-AWARENESS

When we are self-aware, we can notice what is happening in our body—our sensations, emotions, and feelings—as it occurs. This process is sometimes called *present-moment awareness*. You cultivate this present-moment awareness by simply noticing what is happening to you in the current moment, without judgment (Kabat-Zinn, 1994). Cultivating self-awareness takes some practice, particularly if you have been numb to your body or have ignored it as a way of coping with difficult sensations or emotions. In this case, you may have become so accustomed to mindlessness that self-awareness doesn't come naturally. To illustrate what mindlessness involves, ask yourself whether you've ever driven home and not remembered any of the trip because your mind had meandered off into some preoccupation. If you've had that experience—and chances are, you have—that's the opposite of being self-aware.

Through the yoga-based skills in this book, you (and your clients) will learn how to develop self-awareness, or mindfulness, as you pay attention in a specific way. Practicing gentle movement and breathing will help you to reconnect with your body and to notice its needs in a kinder, gentler, and more timely way, both physically and emotionally. Noticing sensations and feelings in the body as they are happening in the moment is the embodiment of present-moment experience.

A note of clarity here: Sometimes the word *mindfulness* and the word *yoga* are used as if they are separate things. However, if yoga is not mindful, then it is not yoga as I understand yoga. I make this point because I have taken classes that were called *yoga* but that were not mindful at all. There was no attention to the breath or to the present-moment experience, or even to what it meant to honor the limits of one's body. Therein lies the confusion about what the two words mean.

The importance of self-awareness is well-illustrated through the concepts of *proprioception* and *interoception*. *Proprioception* refers to awareness of one's own body in space. It is knowing how far we are from other objects so we don't bump into them, correctly judging going up and down steps so we don't fall, and correctly judging distance when backing up our car. It is sometimes referred to as the sixth sense. *Interoception* refers to how we sense, or are aware of, the inner workings of our body—things such as our sensations, feelings, and emotions. An example of interoception is when we are aware of the depth of our own breathing or the sensation of needing to use the restroom (before the need is immediate). It can also involve being aware of any fatigue we are feeling before extreme exhaustion sets in and renders us nonfunctional. Like proprioception, interoception is sometimes referred to as one of the senses (see Figure 1).

While proprioception and interoception may seem organic, they often do not come to us naturally. Trauma can be an especially significant interrupter to proprioception and interoception (Payne, Levine, & Crane-Godreau, 2015). When we forget to honor some of our body's basic needs—such as eating, moving our body every thirty to sixty minutes, or going to the bathroom when we need to, to name just a few—we give ourselves the message that we cannot be trusted to take care of these basic needs. In turn, our body's whispers increase in volume to make itself heard. The good news is that once we realize we are not attuning to the natural functions of the body, we can build the skills needed to develop this awareness. And increased awareness leads to increased proprioception and interoception, which in turn, leads to more health and vitality.

7. LEARN EMOTION REGULATION

When we regularly practice self-care and self-awareness, we can enhance emotion regulation, which is the ability to reset our equilibrium after experiencing intense feelings. The ability to reset is usually what we all want for ourselves and those around us. However, when people struggle with emotion regulation, they find it difficult to come back down to their emotion baseline. When I was growing up in rural Australia, we used the expression, "He always has a bee in his bonnet" to

Figure 1. Proprioception & Interoception: The Sixth and Seventh Senses.
© 2018 Susan McCulley. Used with permission.

describe this experience. Imagine here, the image of a person madly and haphazardly swatting at a tiny bee. Unless you have a severe allergy to bees, the flailing is disproportionate to the situation at hand. Perhaps you have experienced this agitation yourself or seen it in a loved one. Everything seems to bother them. They experience an internal disturbance that manifests through their tone of voice (frantic or high-pitched voice), facial expression (flat or angry), and behavioral reactions (acting out rather than exhibiting a measured response).

In contrast, the essence of emotion regulation involves noticing an emotion *in the moment as it occurs*. The regulating part is about how you give outward expression to that emotion in a way that makes you socially aware of its impact. In an emotionally literate world, we should be able to identify up to forty emotions, both in ourselves and others (Brown, 2018). At first blush, thirty to forty sounded like a lot to me. But when I took out a pen and paper and started naming emotions that I had felt in the last few weeks, I was relieved to come up with ninety. Still, I realize I have to work at identifying emotions in others.

We are not born with the ability to emotionally regulate but learn how to do so by watching others model and express their emotions. **The general emotional climate in which someone was raised—including whether their caregiver validated, accepted, or empathized with their feelings—has a particularly big impact on emotion regulation.** A calm, loving environment is likely to have placed fewer demands on one's ability to regulate than an environment filled with chaos and conflict.

The term *emotion regulation* is sometimes used interchangeably with *self-regulation*. Both terms are part of social and emotional learning (SEL), a term used in educational settings to describe a type of learning that is different from learning how to add and subtract or to construct a grammatically-correct sentence. Many states, with Illinois leading the way, have adopted SEL standards in school curricula, just as there are standards in all core subjects. The following is an example of such a standard from the Illinois State Board of Education.

Imagine if these standards were being taught and modeled in every state. Imagine if teachers took the time (and many do) to identify and manage their own emotions and behaviors and then modeled this behavior to their students. What if we had teachers and students recognize and inventory their personal qualities and identify their external supports? What if we valued

SAMPLE SEL STANDARD

Goal: Develop self-awareness and self-management skills to achieve school and life success.

Standards:

1. Identify and manage one's emotions and behaviors.

2. Recognize personal qualities and external supports.

3. Demonstrate skills related to achieving personal goals.

understanding ourselves in this way as much as we value teaching literacy and basic math? The emotional climate of our schools has and will change for the better as SEL becomes embedded in each state's educational system.

As therapists, we can be a regulating force for our clients until they are able to do it for themselves. We can help them identify and learn to emotionally regulate through gentle moment and the breath, which are key to the foundations of this work and the reason I am finally writing this book. I have identified my own emotion dysregulation and learned to use and apply these skills for myself. This growth and recognition have been mutually beneficial for me and my family.

8. PRIORITIZE SLEEP

It is fascinating to me that a third of our day is spent doing nothing but sleeping—or what *appears* to be nothing. In fact, there are several internal processes that occur during sleep, including extensive cell repair and detoxification. Given that the body is very busy during our down time, it would be hard to overstate that sleep is deeply restorative to our mind and body. Yet we are often cavalier about getting enough sleep because we live in a culture that prizes busyness, multitasking, and overworking. We wear our weariness like a badge of honor. In turn, our sleep has been steadily declining. In fact, in 1850, Americans used to sleep an average of nine and half hours per night. By 1950, that number had decreased to eight hours per night (Tan, 2000).

We joke about, and sometimes prize, how little sleep we get and rarely praise the person who took a nap or went to bed at 9 p.m. The average person gets less than seven hours of sleep each night even though current recommendations indicate that we need at least eight to function optimally. I myself struggled in a state of exhaustion for over twenty years. Admittedly, parenthood alone contributed to much of the exhaustion I felt, but it was also due to my tendency to constantly push myself. This tendency often consisted of working into the night after the kids had gone to bed. I still struggle with pulling the plug on my day and finding a suitable stopping point but following a routine has helped tremendously. I also now have some felt experience of what it is like to *not* be exhausted, and I function much better physically and mentally as a result. My pain levels have dropped, my inflammation has reduced, my anxiety is lower, and my thinking is clearer. It took me two years, but I finally cleaned up my sleep hygiene by prioritizing and ritualizing my sleep habits.

There are compelling reasons to sleep more. In fact, if I were required to focus on one thing for the rest of my yoga teaching days, it would be on helping people sleep better and making sleep a priority. Perhaps it doesn't sound like much, but in doing so, I believe we would all be smarter, thinner, and richer. Why? Think of all the zoned-out screen time, mindless eating, and online purchases that tempt you when your capacity to exercise self-control is *done* for the day. This isn't exactly weakness per se; it is called being tired at the end of the day like most other humans. And any willpower that remains is at its weakest capacity.

Recently, when I was travelling internationally to see my family, I was feeling the effects of jet lag, and it triggered a memory of "this is how you used to feel on a regular basis." My biggest regret is not making changes and cleaning up my act sooner. *But I didn't know what I didn't know.* It feels a little embarrassing to admit, but I do much better on nine hours of sleep per night. Yes, that's right, nine hours. I know this much sleep is a lot (after all, who has that kind of time!), but it is more doable than you think. I double dog dare you to give it a try.

Sleep Challenge

What if, for several days in a row, you slept until you were done? Really done. As in, you literally cannot sleep anymore. You wake up without an alarm, and you stay in bed until there is no more sleep left in you. *But, Joanne, I can't do that. I have a job to go to, children to care for.* Okay, then try going to bed an hour earlier for several nights in a row and see what happens. How does it feel? The alternative is counting the cost of accumulative exhaustion to your health and well-being. It is possible that getting more sleep may be the answer to why you feel so crappy much of the time. It is worth a try, and there is no downside.

If everything I've discussed so far isn't enough to get you to bed earlier, think of your immune system. At the time of going to press with this book, we are in the midst of a global pandemic. Over 300,000 people in the US have lost their lives to COVID-19. Never has there been a more important time in recent history to support one's immune system. Having a healthy immune system is our first line of defense, and a sleep-deprived body has a much harder time fighting disease. This is because sleep deprivation reduces the release of cytokines, which are small proteins that help regulate your immune system (Breus, 2020). In fact, people who get less than six of hours of sleep each night are more than four times as likely to catch a cold than those who get quality rest (Prather, Janicki-Deverts, Hall, & Cohen, 2015). This is a compelling reason to go to bed earlier; it's likely your health depends upon it.

In order to get restful sleep each night, you should maintain consistent sleep and wake times (going to bed and getting up at the same time every day), keep a cool bedroom temperature (about 68 degrees Fahrenheit, or 20 degrees Celsius, is optimal), and limit screen time thirty minutes prior to sleep (Walker, 2017). If you struggle with sleep apnea, it is important to address that as well, so you improve sleep quality and carbon dioxide absorption during sleep (McKeown, 2015). Your quality of life is likely to improve significantly as a result.

9. FIND CONNECTION

While the practices in this book are effective when done independently, there is a benefit to doing them in a group because it promotes connection and prosocial behavior. We acknowledge one another, knowing that we are breathing the same air and that we are all on a journey of healing. In fact, the National Health System (NHS) in the U.K. is starting to recommend yoga to more patients under the realm of *social prescribing*, which is the notion that individuals who maintain an active social life experience enhanced emotional and physical well-being compared to those who socially isolate. In fact, interacting with others can reduce blood pressure, enhance cognitive functioning, and (depending on the specific social activity) improve fitness levels.

The NHS recognizes that yoga meets this critical human need for connection. I make this point in every class I teach. *Here we are, moving and breathing together. We are connected.* If I am working with a group, we may even give each other a high five or at least an air high five. As unsophisticated or amusing as it may sound, doing air high fives never fails to elicit a positive response or elevate someone's mood. As humans, we are wired for connection. It is a biological imperative (Porges, 2017). Imagine a group of male veterans over sixty, in wheelchairs, sitting around smiling and high fiving each other in their weekly chair yoga class. While this image may seem unlikely to you, it is a constant in my world of teaching. It is truly beautiful to witness, and it demonstrates the power of connection in promoting prosocial behavior. I couldn't make this stuff up.

I was recently in a meeting with a physician and researcher who is very interested in studying how yoga can help reduce the symptoms of PTSD in veterans. Although he suspected that a gentle, breath-focused yoga class would reduce PTSD symptoms, his concern was whether veterans would want to do yoga. I simply smiled and asked if he had time to come to my classes at the VA that day so he could see for himself. The veterans I see *want* to do yoga. That's what happens when you, as a clinician, create an atmosphere of welcome and invitation, alongside empathy and compassion, offering respect and dignity. The practice becomes hard to resist, and clients come to realize that quietly and confidently moving their body leads to shifts in mood and well-being. Seeing and feeling this shift is usually enough to make even the hardest of hearts give yoga a try. Your role is to show up for yourself and for your clients. When you show up this way, the connection happens. It is one of being *with* another.

There is tremendous power in our relationships with others to both hurt and heal (van der Kolk, 2014). The chair yoga groups I teach are remarkable examples of how relationships can heal. When we offer hospitality and community to one another, even when we are simply breathing the same air together, magic happens. Of course, what looks like magic isn't magic at all. After reading this book and putting it into practice, you too will understand the magic that ancient yogis discovered and how modern neuroscience now explains it.

10. KEEP HYDRATED

If your major liquid intake comes from tea, coffee, soda, or juice, you may want to stop reading right now and drink a big glass of water. Drinking water keeps every system in your body functioning properly. Not only does water carry nutrients and oxygen to your cells, but it also removes bacteria from your bladder, promotes digestion, and prevents constipation. Staying hydrated also stabilizes your heart rate and normalizes blood pressure (Godman, 2016). There is plenty of evidence demonstrating our need for copious amounts of water each day, and there are plenty of resources to refer to and to even help remind you to drink water.[*] Although it is possible to drink too much water, many more people are underhydrated than overhydrated.

For example, I once worked with a client who was depressed and in chronic pain. She was willing to make some small changes to her daily routine, like the foundational principles listed here, and the impact of increasing daily hydration was one that was felt almost immediately. She had mistakenly

---

[*] This is the clearest explanation I have found as to what happens if you don't drink water: https://youtu.be/9iMGFqMmUFs. Here is also a handy calculator that tells you how much water to drink according to what activity you are doing: https://www.camelbak.com/en/hydrated/hydration-calculator.

believed that soda counted as hydration until I asked her to read the label on the can. Sugar (or high fructose corn syrup—sugar in another form) was the second ingredient, followed various unidentifiable and unpronounceable ingredients. She ditched the soda and began drinking water instead, and this simple change caused immediate changes in her mood and energy the next day. It reinforced the importance of staying hydrated to live well. My recommendation is that you also educate yourself and become mindful about what you put in your body. You should view any long list of ingredients as a potential red flag. They may not be good ingredients to ingest, regardless of whether they have been FDA approved. *I am just saying.*

To stay hydrated, you should drink six to eight glasses of water per day. And don't wait until you are thirsty. If you wait until you're thirsty to drink, that means you're already dehydrated. If you are worried that drinking too much water will make you need to use the bathroom multiple times at night, then frontload your water intake in the morning—beginning when you wake up. For example, each morning I drink twenty to thirty ounces of room temperature water followed by about ten ounces of warm water.

Ayurvedic medicine, which is a sister science to yoga, also recommends drinking room temperature water before each meal—at least fifteen minutes prior—and not during the meal. Doing so hydrates the lining of the stomach so it can more easily absorb the nutrients from your food, whereas drinking water during the meal dilutes the digestive juices. If you feel like you must drink something during your meal, try *sipping* warm water. In addition, you should consider buying a plastic-free reusable water bottle and carry it with you wherever you go. Doing so is not only in the interest of helping the planet, but it will remind you to sip water throughout the day. Drinking enough water each day is pretty easy to implement, and you may be astounded at the difference it will make to your physical and mental well-being.

SUMMARY

These ten foundational principles are essential for understanding how and why the recommended practices in this book work. Think of these principles as a checklist to live by and work by. I print them out and carry them with me so I can look at them as daily reminders. This way I can be intentional about my well-being. Well-being does not happen of its own accord or in a vacuum. These things happen as a result of daily practice that leads to habit-forming behavior and thinking. Habits run our lives; make your habits life-giving ones.

10 Foundational Principles

1. Link Breath and Movement

2. Only Move in Your Pain-Free Range of Motion

3. Make Friends with Your Body

4. Slow Down

5. Practice Self-Care

6. Develop Self-Awareness

7. Learn Emotion Regulation

8. Prioritize Sleep

9. Find Connection

10. Keep Hydrated

CHAPTER 3
TRAUMA-INFORMED YOGA: THE BASICS

This chapter, which is intended primarily for yoga teachers, provides additional information regarding the basics of trauma-informed practice as it applies to yoga, as well as a description of different standards and guidelines that vary across yoga organizations. Although the focus of this book is largely geared toward therapists, my hope is that the tools I present here will be a starting point for you as a yoga teacher (or a yoga teacher-in-training) to become trauma-informed in your teaching and to understand yoga as a powerful tool that can change lives. You have the ability to either help someone heal or make things worse, and knowing the difference is extremely important.

YOGA STANDARDS

There are two different yoga organizations in the U.S. that speak to standards. However, they are unrelated and have different missions, which can sometimes be confusing to yoga teachers. The first is the Yoga Alliance (YA), which was founded in the late 1990s and is a national, voluntary, member-based organization serving yoga teachers and yoga schools. In 2018, YA began a review of its standards and credentialing process through the Standards Review Project, which has resulted from a growing realization that most entry level yoga teacher trainings, like the 200-hour level, are just that—a place to begin—because they only require the minimum number of hours deemed necessary to safely teach a yoga class. The number of individuals participating in these 200-hour level trainings has likely increased as a function of the growing number of people taking yoga classes, which increased over fifty percent between 2012 and 2016 (Yoga Journal and Yoga Alliance, 2016). Currently, there are 90,400 registered yoga teachers and over 6,200 registered yoga schools in the U.S. The trainees who complete such programs are deemed to be registered yoga teachers—RYT 200 or RYT 500—depending on the length of the training.

The other organization is the International Association of Yoga Therapists (IAYT), whose mission is to establish yoga as a recognized and respected therapy. The association views yoga therapy as a practice that adapts "to the needs of people with specific or persistent health problems not usually addressed in a group class." In 2017, the IAYT introduced a certification process specifically for yoga therapists. To date, there are nearly 4,000 certified yoga therapists. The credentialing process is extensive and substantial, requiring 850 hours of yoga education and an additional 600 hours with clients, plus specialized knowledge of specific health populations. As of 2019, IAYT has over 5,000 individual members from over fifty countries, as well as over 170 member schools, fifty of which are yoga therapy accredited training programs.

The scope of practice within both IAYT and YA regarding yoga therapy and yoga teaching has been hotly debated for many years. Each organization has a different perspective for different reasons. Their websites provide a plethora of information to better understand where you may fit as a yoga teacher. I have a foot in each camp. I am an RYT 500 with YA and a certified yoga therapist with IAYT. Being a yoga teacher with a mental health background, I find that both organizations have merit and appeal in a world trying to make sense of how and where yoga fits in terms of health treatments and well-being. My interest in trauma-informed practice has taken me on a journey to seek as much information and education specific to my work as possible. Trauma is now prevalent enough that the odds of having a traumatized person in any yoga class are high. For example, in a class of twenty yoga students, it is likely that at least one or two individuals will have a history of trauma, and even four or more individuals in higher-risk populations and locations (Cook-Cottone et al., 2017).

For this reason alone, I believe it is highly advisable to include some best practices in trauma-informed yoga in all yoga teacher trainings, even (or especially) at the 200-hour level. As of the writing of this book, instruction in trauma-informed yoga is not included at the 200-hour level, but I hope this will change in the future. Although YA's training quality work group has identified a need for specialized knowledge about trauma, it does not distinguish between treating trauma and being trauma-informed as a universal precaution, as I am suggesting.

IF IN DOUBT, JUST SLOW DOWN

If you have some yoga teacher training in your background, you may already be familiar with some of the practices I am offering in this book. Do not be put off by their simplicity or gentleness. I was first introduced to the phrase "Gentle is the new advanced" by J. Brown, and this sentiment was echoed by one of my teachers, Kristine Kaoverii Weber, whose tagline is the "slow yoga revolution." Now, twenty years into my journey as a yoga teacher, I think I understand what that means. On my own website, I call myself the "slow-movement maven" as a reminder that slow movement is key to restoring the nervous system. If you are a yoga teacher and decide to take on and study the gentle and restorative aspects of yoga—even though you may have been trained in a different style, such as vinyasa-based yoga—be forewarned that you may be told that you are misrepresenting yoga. Do not be dissuaded. The overwhelming evidence presented in this book demonstrates otherwise.

As counterintuitive as it seems, there is nothing easy about moving slowly, particularly if your usual practice and teaching are more along the lines of vinyasa yoga or a hot, athletic practice. Indeed, the practices in this book may be quite difficult for you because they are slow, or after trying these practices, you may initially feel no effect because your nervous system is used to constant movement. And that's okay. My request is that you stay open to the possibility that your own nervous system needs some regulation. I know I often masked my physical and emotional pain with busyness, a fast-paced life, and fast-paced movement. In doing so, I didn't have to feel things in the way that slow movement encourages. I encourage you to be your own laboratory. Your body will give you feedback, even if that is initially a "WTF" (woman turning fifty) reaction, which is a pretty good approximation of my own initial reaction to slow movement. Slow, trauma-informed yoga eventually became a catalyst for healing my own childhood trauma.

Yoga teachers may also want to lengthen the practices offered here. Perhaps one practice will inspire you to build around it. Or you may find merit in combining many practices and establish a slower pace for an entire class. Something I hear quite often from yoga teachers is that, when introducing these materials, they ripped right through five practices in five minutes and then ran out of material. Instead, please recognize that less is more. Not only is it a practice to move slowly, it is a practice unto itself to teach slowly and mindfully and to slow your own breathing. To be sure, the benefits of sixty-, seventy-five- and ninety-minute yoga classes can be great. But that's not why I have written this book. I am still amazed by the calming benefits of what five to ten minutes of gentle movement and breathing can do for someone. Five minutes doesn't seem too much to ask of a busy person to support their own well-being, right? Finding a slow pace that works for you will go a long way toward helping you find your way into slowness and a sense of ease and self-regulation. We get better at things we practice.

If you want to increase your awareness of the benefits of a slower-paced yoga class, I recommend taking a restorative yoga class for yourself. Feel the difference, comparing the state of your mind and body before class with your well-being after. Notice whether this act of surrender was hard or

Hannah's Story: When Slow is Good

It was hot—nearly ninety degrees at 8:30 in the morning—but it was Cancun, and I was on vacation, at least after I taught two yoga classes. It was my first day there, and I had only *one* student show up to my first yoga class (apart from my husband). Her name was Hannah, and I knew our time would be interesting when she told me she usually did practices that had the words *boot camp* in them. She was a strong, tough woman. I explained right up front that what I teach is slow, gentle, and breath focused, and I paused for emphasis to see if she would run away screaming something like, "That's not yoga!" But she didn't. Instead, she said, "You know, as I was doing my devotion by the pool this morning, I realized that I might need some yoga. It will be fine." Wow. She sounded like she had slowed down enough (she *was* on vacation after all) to gain some insight about what her body needed. And with that, I started class... doing slow, gentle, restorative yoga. At the end, as we sat almost knee to knee with our hands in *angeli mudra* (heart center), I heard myself saying, "Be still and know."

As I bowed to her, I saw a look of gratitude and tears welling in her eyes. She was silent and very calm. I didn't probe her because I generally try and refrain from asking how someone is doing in those moments and just let them *be* in the experience. If they want to share with words, they can, but I am not going to ask a question to provoke an answer. A few minutes later, she told me that more people should do yoga so they can remember their humanity as human beings and not human *doings*. The rough edges and toughness had melted away. She was replaced by a softer, slower, and even kinder self. The shift was palpable, and she left class in a floaty (but grounded) sort of way. I whispered to my husband, "I live for these moments."

easy, and what made it so. I am not suggesting you give up flowing or athletic practices if you like them and if you can do them with appropriate awareness and without pain. I am simply suggesting that there is so much more to the yoga experience. And if you think that gentle, restorative, or chair practices are limited to the infirm and elderly, think again. We *all* can benefit from gentle, restorative practices, although we may not yet know that we need them. These practices allow our nervous system to regulate as we calm ourselves down, energize ourselves, and find stillness.

Although restorative yoga has a restful and peaceful quality to it, it doesn't necessarily feel restful when you are first learning a pose. For example, there is a yoga pose called "Downward Dog" that can be challenging at first, particularly if it is unfamiliar. It requires putting your hands and feet on the floor (or at least parts of them) and folding your body at the hip to make an upside-down V-shape with your hips toward the ceiling. The pose requires engaging a lot of muscles in order to stay in the pose for more than a breath or two. But with time and practice, it gets easier, and dare I say, even restful. It builds our capacity to tolerate using muscles in a more challenging way than certain actions require of us, like standing or walking. In the same way that we can mindfully challenge our muscles, we can also expand our emotional capacity, including our ability to tolerate difficult emotions, such as grief, sadness, and shame. Physically slowing down creates space for such emotions to arise and find their expression as a common part of our human experience.

In my early years of learning yoga, I studied with a teacher who would say things such as, "I am not here to make you comfortable." I was puzzled by this comment for a long time. As a mental health therapist and yoga teacher, I was always trying to make people more comfortable amidst the sometimes-miserable challenges they were facing, although I know that making people comfortable is not usually the goal of therapy. However, the practices in this book can help us find real comfort and consolation as our nervous system becomes regulated and more even-keeled. In her book, *Dare to Lead*, Brené Brown (2018) talks about the importance of identifying real comfort, as opposed to things that give us a temporary quick fix, like comfort eating or numbing out with alcohol and drugs. The more we experience true comfort, the more likely we will turn to that practice when we need it.

In my own experience, I was able to identify that my yoga practice brings me real comfort. But it wasn't always so. It was very challenging for me to learn most of the breathing practices in this book. I did not understand just how dysregulated my nervous system was until I tried doing a whole hour of breathing practices (which I don't recommend—start small and build from there). I observed that my mind got very busy, and then I promptly fell asleep to cope with the overload. In class. On multiple occasions. Oops.

I continued to teach yoga for several years without understanding, or even knowing about, the connection-to-the-breath aspect of yoga. Upon reflection, perhaps my body wasn't ready to learn the powerful yogic concept of resting, often referred to as a state of being relaxed in the body and alert in the mind. However, one day, something shifted, and I felt relaxed, yet alert. I wept as I recognized my own gap between knowing and doing. I had been teaching yoga for several years by then, yet relaxing wasn't something I had made room for in my life. Doesn't it sound like that confession could be in a book called *True Confessions of a High-Strung Yoga Teacher*? The irony is not lost on me. I have learned that we often are repelled by things we need the most. Or as psychologist Dr. Albert Wong says, "We teach what we need to learn" (2020). So please be kind and compassionate to yourself if you are resonating with my experience.

In the following section, I lay out an overview of key concepts to embody in your teaching in order to make your work as a yoga teacher trauma-informed. These concepts are simply a place to begin your exploration of trauma-informed yoga practice. Perhaps you already are doing, practicing, or teaching these things in your class without even realizing it. Or perhaps you have trained in a yoga lineage or with a teacher who has a deep working knowledge of trauma and how it resides in the body. I encourage you to seek out workshops, trainings, and books that will fill in any gaps in your knowledge about teaching in a way that is trauma-informed or trauma-sensitive. As a yoga teacher, you have a responsibility to your students, first, to do no harm. Are you equipped to do that? Reading this book and incorporating the foundational principles into your teaching and practice will be a helpful start.

BASICS OF TRAUMA-INFORMED PRACTICE

Choice. Always give choices using invitational language. Giving someone choices regarding a pose or breathing exercise should also include the freedom to *not* do the pose or breathing exercise at all. This way, you help students learn to trust their own judgment about what is appropriate for them to do in that moment. The following are some examples of invitational language:

- "I invite you to…" (instead of "I want you to…")
- "If you want to, join me in raising your arms on your next inhale."
- "Would you like to try _____?"
- "I invite you to sit in a comfortable position."
- "If you would like, join me in linking your breath to your movement. Inhale, lift your arms. Exhale, lower them."
- "As you start to notice your breathing, feel free to have your eyes open or closed, whichever feels more comfortable to you."

Knowing the suitability of a yoga pose or breathing exercise often comes from practicing and being able to feel the effect of that practice. Noticing the effect of a pose or breathing practice is particularly helpful in certain situations. For example, if you want to use a calming practice to prepare for bed and a good night's rest, choose a practice that has made you calm in the past rather than a practice that has energized you. There are no hard and fast rules that always apply, mostly because each person's nervous system responds differently to different practices. As you gain experience in the practices, you start to know yourself better. You become aware of what calms you and what energizes you.

Emphasizing a client's choice is particularly important if you are working in an institutional setting, like a VA, or in a restrictive setting like a juvenile detention center, where people are used to being told what to do. In these cases, I suggest explicitly acknowledging the choice they have in the practice of yoga by saying something like:

Perhaps you have been exposed to an environment where following orders or mandatory rules are the norm. Yoga is different from that. I cannot make you do anything, let alone move and breathe in a particular way, unless you want to. In this class today, you have my permission and complete freedom to decide what you want to do or not to do. You can engage or not engage, for any reason. Yoga is about self-care and self-awareness. You are the expert on you and your needs, not me. I am here to guide you with helpful instruction. Of course, I practice yoga myself, so I know its power and the effect it has had on my own mind and body, so I am hoping you will give it a try. But it is completely up to you to decide what is best for you today. And I will honor and respect your choice.

The use of such emphatic language, repeated over time, gives people the confidence to tune in to themselves and to start trusting that they can make good decisions for themselves, even if that is simply deciding whether they want to lift their arms over their head and breathe. If you can point them to their own agency—highlighting that they do have some control over some things—you are headed in the right direction.

Your Audience. Consider the population of people you are teaching. Are you teaching in a yoga studio in the suburbs? Or are you teaching in a juvenile detention center? Or perhaps an after-school program in the inner city? Context matters. The practices in this book will work across a very diverse range of environments. Your job is to know your people and to educate and equip yourself to be culturally competent to teach the people in front of you.

Your Position in the Room. Put your back to the door, not theirs. Someone with a history of trauma often wants to see where the exits are or to sit near them.

Awareness. Read the body language of the people around you. How are they breathing? Over time, you can train your eyes and mind to notice the subtleties of someone's breathing. It is helpful to keep in mind that you may be in a room of highly anxious individuals. Often, they will need to move frequently to dissipate some of their nervous energy. Although slow movement may be challenging, any movement will help and will eventually allow them to enjoy a slower, quiet practice. If someone is mostly quiet and has a flat affect, then start with a quiet practice, like breathing, and build to more energizing breathing and movement to elevate the mood. In LifeForce Yoga, we call this *meeting the mood*.

Pause. Practice creating an intentional space of silence after you say something. It is not necessary to fill up every space with words. Take time to pause, and pause often. Let silence be your friend.

Tone of Voice. When you speak, think of thick, sweet honey coating your vocal cords. As an example, notice how you usually talk to small children and animals. Often, your intonation, pitch, and pace softens—that is the tone of voice that will be helpful for you to use. Record yourself talking so you know how you sound. Do you sound angry even when you are not (or don't realize you are)? The state of your nervous system affects your tone of voice, and it is very hard to sound genuinely calm and kind if you are not feeling calm and kind. Being able to identify your inner state and what you need to calm this state before you teach a class continues to be of paramount importance. What works for you will depend on your life stage and circumstances. For some, it involves taking deep breaths during the two-minute walk from the car to the studio before teaching. For others, it may involve taking at least an hour before a class to plan, refresh, and focus. The point here is to do the best you can with what you have available. Sometimes that will be a whole hour and sometimes not. I always like to have a back-up plan or my "tried and true" practices if my usual prep has not worked or has been hijacked in some way.

Your Own Presence. Make sure you are present and accounted for every class you teach. That means getting enough rest, staying hydrated, fueling your body with proper nutrition, and so forth. In polyvagal terms, it means being in a ventral vagal state, which is a state of relaxation and social engagement (see chapter 4). Other people's nervous systems will take their cues from your nervous system. Therefore, if there is only one person in the room in a ventral vagal state, let it be you (Dana, 2018).

No Hands-On Adjustments. Learn how to use your body language, gestures, and vocal tone to offer comfort or empathy. Use your words, and perhaps demonstrate using your own body, to show someone how to adjust themselves even if you trained in a lineage that teaches hands-on adjustments. For example, if you see someone's face contort when they try to follow your cue to lift both hands over their head, it might be helpful to say (and to remind them), "Let's lift our arms to the natural stopping point, in our pain-free range of motion." And then demonstrate moving your arms only halfway. A follow-up cue may be, "Soften your jaw and your face muscles. Find your breath. Do a little less if you are not breathing smoothly." Or, as yoga teacher and author Max Strom (2017) likes to say, "Relax your face like you are on vacation… for the rest of your life."

Slowness. Slow down your movement, your breath, and the pace of your speech. Create a vibe characterized by "We have all the time we need" versus "Let's hurry up and relax." When we slow down, it helps create present-moment awareness, and this awareness is the key to learning so that change becomes possible (Doige, 2017).

SUMMARY

The skilled and competent teaching of yoga has much to offer, both physiologically and psychologically. As Kristine Kaoverii Weber states:

> *Lifestyle medicine is beginning to be recognized as the solution to the chronic conditions that plague our culture. Yoga, as a holistic system, is perhaps the finest iteration of lifestyle medicine. At a workshop last year, I asked Harvard researcher Sat Bir Khalsa if he thinks that yoga is one solution to the chronic disease epidemic. He said to me, "No, it's not one solution, it is THE solution." (2019)*

Weber goes on to say, "Good yoga teaching is, essentially, an antidote to so much of what ails us in Western cultures. And if you are good at teaching yoga, you are a professional with a very valuable and unique skill" (2019). I echo Weber's sentiments, and I offer these statements as encouragement to continue to teach and learn. At the same time, stay open to the knowledge that there is so much more to yoga than what is covered in a 200-hour teacher training. See the resources section for training materials and references for your own self-study.

CHAPTER 4
POLYVAGAL THEORY ESSENTIALS

During the process of writing this book, a book which focuses primarily on practice, I came to realize that polyvagal theory is important enough not to just mention, but to unpack and to devote an entire chapter to it. At the risk of offending experts on the vagus nerve and neurologists who may read this chapter, I am going to attempt to simplify a complicated topic. I offer my insights in the spirit of giving you some ways to understand what we mean when we talk about the autonomic nervous system and its various pathways, including why this scientific understanding can contribute to trauma-informed practice for those of us who are primarily clinicians and not researchers. My understanding is from that of a clinical perspective. My body understood the theory way ahead of my cognitive capacities, and I was able to experience the joy of being in a *ventral vagal* state, the energy of being in a *sympathetic nervous system* state, and the collapse of being in a *dorsal vagal* state before I ever had the technical words to describe it.

My journey to understanding the polyvagal theory occurred by sitting through many explanations, lectures, and seminars and by reading several books and articles on the topic. And here's what usually happens when I've made such efforts to attend to material of a complex nature: My interest is piqued by the exotic sounding terminology. I sit up straighter and maybe even lean in a little with my notepad and pen poised. At some level, probably in my gut, I get the gist of what I am hearing. But throw in one too many scientific terms without clear explanation or without connection as to why polyvagal theory matters in a yoga class or therapy session, and my eyes begin to glaze over. I can no longer listen or take in the complex information. I somehow become stuck, and the information no longer gets through. I am in information overload. If this scenario has ever happened to you, I'd like to help you get unstuck without being overwhelmed. At the same time, please know that there is more to the polyvagal theory than I can present here. What I can offer is a summary and an overview of the theory and suggestions about how to apply the theory to practice.

Once you understand the theory, you can identify what state your nervous system is in at any given moment. With this important information, you can be a regulating resource for your clients and those around you. My own knowledge of the autonomic nervous system, and of polyvagal theory, has become foundational to my understanding of why yoga works to calm, activate, or rebalance the nervous system. More specifically, the theory has given me language to explain the mechanism of how and why embodied practices, such as yoga, are powerful tools for self-regulating. It's really all about connection and how we access the feeling of safety in our bodies. The theory provides a foundation upon which my yoga skills and knowledge rest. My objective in this chapter is for you to develop a working knowledge of the polyvagal theory too.

I encourage you to bring your own intellectual curiosity to this complex yet compelling theory so you can gain more understanding of why your work as a therapist is so important. This knowledge will allow you to fairly accurately select a practice that will *support* or *shift* the state of your nervous system. Successfully achieving these shifts consistently over time may change how you work with your clients. But even more importantly, it may change how you live your life. In fact, knowing the theory may confirm some of the more intuitive hunches you feel as you practice the tools for yourself.

Before we dive into the details of polyvagal theory, I ask that you give this chapter your full attention. Find a comfortable chair to support your body, and turn off your cell phone to support your brain's ability to focus and settle in. As you read, I hope that you deepen a sense of connection to yourself and others as the theory becomes more of a concrete reality. I urge you to take in everything the polyvagal theory has to offer with an open mind and open heart. Perhaps take a deep breath, inhaling and exhaling, connect to yourself, feel your feet on the floor in the here and now, and keep reading.

POLYVAGAL THEORY BASICS

The polyvagal theory, which was originally developed by Stephen Porges in 1994, provides us with an understanding of how our body assesses and responds to cues of safety and danger in our environment. In particular, the theory proposes that the way we respond and react to threats in our environment reflects the evolutionary hierarchy of our autonomic nervous system, which comprises a three-part structure.

The evolutionarily oldest part of this system is the *dorsal vagal* circuit, which is part of the parasympathetic nervous system. The dorsal vagal circuit protects us from life-threatening situations by shutting down the body to conserve energy, and it does so by sending the body into a state of collapse. For example, some animals feign death to preserve their life. Variations of this behavior can be seen in humans. For example, we become numb, dissociate, or feel paralyzed with fear in response to some overwhelming threat from which there seems no escape. Our body has the ability to override all other systems and shut down in order to preserve our life. This adaptive survival response explains trauma reactions. Although individuals who have experienced trauma are often disappointed or ashamed in the body's response (e.g., "Why didn't I defend myself?"), polyvagal theory explains that *not* fighting or defending oneself may have been life preserving. This fact alone is cause to celebrate the body's strong survival mechanism.

The next system to evolve was the *sympathetic nervous system*, which is designed to mobilize our body for action through movement and active engagement. In particular, the sympathetic nervous system activates the body's fight-or-flight response, which propels us to run toward the threat head on (fight) or to run away from it (flight). It does so by releasing a flood of stress hormones into the body, like adrenaline and cortisol, that provide the body with a burst of energy.

Finally, the newest system to evolve is the *ventral vagal* circuit, which is also part of the parasympathetic nervous system. This ventral vagal circuit, which is only found in mammals, is also known as the social engagement system because it provides us with a sense of safety and connection in the context of relationships. This is the part of our autonomic nervous system that provides us with the ability to co-regulate, which is the "mutual regulation of physiological states between individuals" (Porges, 2017, p. 9). We regulate our nervous systems when we connect with each other. For example, co-regulation occurs when a mother calms an upset child by gently speaking to and rocking the child. This has the reciprocal effect of calming the mother's own nervous system as well. This effect can also occur in relationships with mammals other than humans. Think, for example, of how stroking your cat or dog can be calming for both you and your pet.

The image of the ladder (Figure 2) can help you visualize this hierarchical nature of the autonomic nervous system.

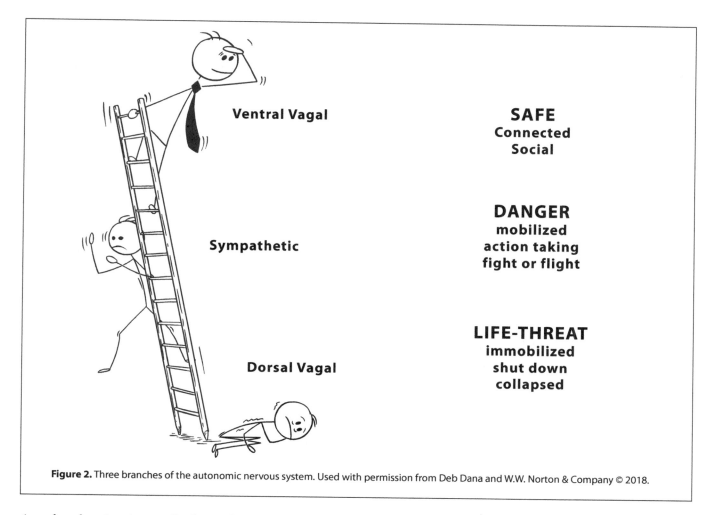

Ventral Vagal

SAFE
Connected
Social

Sympathetic

DANGER
mobilized
action taking
fight or flight

Dorsal Vagal

LIFE-THREAT
immobilized
shut down
collapsed

Figure 2. Three branches of the autonomic nervous system. Used with permission from Deb Dana and W.W. Norton & Company © 2018.

At the beginning of this chapter, when I mentioned my own intellectual struggles in understanding scientific concepts, I described how my body shuts down when I'm overwhelmed by more information than I can take in. This description is the embodiment of what happens to the nervous system when it is in a dorsal vagal state, and an understanding of polyvagal theory helps explain why this response occurs. Before writing this chapter, I was comfortably seated and humming along in a ventral vagal state, feeling calm and just peachy, preparing myself to write. As soon as I reread what I had written, I began to feel anxious about whether I was explaining it "right," and I started shifting into a sympathetic nervous system response. This mobilizing response eventually turned into a feeling of hopelessness, reflecting a dorsal vagal state, because my autonomic nervous system starts to activate (and then tanks) when I think I don't have what it takes to explain polyvagal theory. When this occurs, I attempt to ground and center myself again so I can shift back into a ventral vagal state and continue writing. My example is not unique, as feelings of stress or despair happen to all of us at various points in our life, whether these stressors are small or large, and whether they are real or perceived (Moseley, 2011).

THE "WANDERING" VAGUS NERVE AND THE AUTONOMIC NERVOUS SYSTEM

To understand polyvagal theory, it is necessary to understand the structure of the vagus nerve and how it works with the autonomic nervous system. The vagus nerve, which is the tenth cranial nerve, is sometimes called "the wanderer" because it inhabits (and wanders) the entire length of the torso. It runs down through the brain and into a number of structures, such as the facial muscles, throat, heart, lungs, stomach, and intestines. One of my favorite images of the vagus nerve is a schematic representation by Andreas Vesalius (Figure 3), which I came across in 2016 when I was preparing a self-care workshop for the United Steel Workers Union. I needed an image that told a story and brought the vagus wanderer to life. Since then, I have seen Vesalius's rendition in many publications and presentations. I have yet to find one more captivating than this. It astounds me that he had such understanding of the vagus nerve in the sixteenth century.

As I mentioned in the preceding section, the vagus nerve governs the two distinct pathways of the parasympathetic nervous system: an evolutionarily older unmyelinated branch (*dorsal vagal circuit*) and a newer myelinated branch (*ventral vagal circuit*). Both branches of the vagus nerve work to inhibit sympathetic nervous system activation, though the manner in which they do so differs. The more primitive dorsal vagal branch does so abruptly by shutting the body down into a state of complete immobilization, whereas the newer ventral vagal branch does so in a more calming manner by facilitating social engagement. It is for this reason that the parasympathetic (including both the ventral and dorsal vagal pathways) and sympathetic nervous systems are often described as the body's brake and accelerator, respectively. The sympathetic nervous system serves to speed the body up, and the parasympathetic nervous system serves to slow it down.

Eighty percent of the fibers in the vagus nerve arise from the body and travel toward the brain, and the other twenty percent originate from the brain to the body. This means that the wandering nerve takes cues from what is happening inside the body (that is, how we are feeling), as well as

Figure 3. Illustration of the cranial nerves in *De Humani Corporis Fabrica Libri Septem* (Vesalius, 1543).

what is happening outside of the body (in our environment), to determine our level of felt safety. As humans and social beings, we unconsciously take cues from others' facial expressions, tone of voice, and so forth to decide if another person or situation is safe or not. Porges coined the term *neuroception* to describe this process, and it reflects how our nervous system is constantly scanning our environment for threats, which is an activity that happens beneath conscious awareness. These cues of safety versus threat are most often gleaned from observing the muscles of the face: Is the person in front of me smiling, or is her affect flat? Is his tone of voice soothing, or is it harsh? Neuroception informs our nervous system from such cues, in turn influencing what state we are in.

Importantly, we can learn to recognize the state we are in and eventually influence this state, even toggling between states when necessary. This idea of intentionally changing states is a paradoxical one because the autonomic nervous system is *automatic* in that it operates without our conscious input. However, we can *learn* to exert some control over the autonomic nervous system with practice, and this agency often involves using our breath. Controlling how we breathe is the most immediate way to access and create a change of state in our autonomic nervous system because it improves vagal tone, which is a physiological marker of stress vulnerability (Porges, 2017). It is for this reason that attention to the breath is included in *every* practice in this book.

When we have high vagal tone, our digestion improves, our heart functions optimally, and our mood stabilizes. A toned vagus nerve allows us to switch between parasympathetic and sympathetic nervous system activation, which builds our resilience and connection—both of which are protective factors against trauma. It allows us to "blend" our ventral vagal system with the sympathetic nervous system when we want to mobilize into action in a regulated and functional way. Similarly, it allows us to safely access the dorsal vagal system when we want to be still, quiet, and in a more contemplative state of mind. This contemplative state is a helpful one to cultivate for a meditation or a mindfulness practice. Deb Dana (2018) identifies these ways of being as blended states:

Ventral + sympathetic (healthy) = playful

Ventral + dorsal (healthy) = contemplative/meditative

These are healthy and functional ways we can harness the different branches of the nervous system.

Each of the practices I describe in this book will tone the vagus nerve. At the same time, different practices have different effects on the nervous system. Some practices are calming and soothing (ventral vagal system), some are activating and mobilizing (sympathetic nervous system), and some promote inner stillness and deep rest (dorsal vagal system). Just as we experience different states of the nervous system for different reasons, the practices in this book will affect each individual differently. However, in choosing to do a practice for a *particular* effect, you will notice over time that your response will be more predictable, thereby providing useful information regarding which practice is more appropriate at any given time.

When I am teaching the practices in this book, I usually mention that we will be moving our bodies very gently, and it may not look or feel like much exertion physically. However, I explain that we are working out the nervous system by using the breath and a few key gentle movements. I find the use of the word *workout* useful when working with men, and veterans in particular, despite my view that yoga is not simply a fitness-based activity but part of a wisdom tradition and whole-body practice. The phrase "working out your nervous system" gives them words to assign what they are feeling in their bodies and makes sense of them. I would like to acknowledge and clarify some words. Using the word *workout* and *men* may sound stereotypical. I have spent my entire yoga career trying to bust the stereotype of who does and can do yoga, and instead broadcast the message that all bodies are welcome. However, I still felt it was worth noting what I have observed when working with this population.

THE BODY'S TRAUMA RESPONSE

When real or perceived circumstances trigger feelings of threat or danger, we may feel as if our nervous system is hijacking our body. In reality, we are responding to the signals from the amygdala, which is a primal smoke alarm-like system deep in the brain stem that serves to warn us of danger, whether that danger is real or imagined. These bodily warnings come in various forms—such as sweaty palms, increased heart rate, and heightened emotions—and prepare the body to respond to the danger. These warnings happen outside of conscious awareness; we do not make them happen, and we cannot will them away or talk them into behaving differently.

For individuals with a history of trauma or PTSD, this alert system remains stuck in the past even though the threat has since passed. In turn, the body may overreact at the slightest sign of danger, causing the nervous system to mobilize into defensive actions in response to the perceived threat (sympathetic nervous system response) or to shut down if the threat seems too overwhelming (dorsal vagal response). The body gets stuck in the past although the experience of the trauma is long gone. As Bessel van der Kolk (2014) famously says in his bestselling book by the same title: The body keeps the score. **Trauma resides in the body and cannot simply be *talked* away.**

When clients with a trauma history present to a therapy session, they may acknowledge that there is no actual threat to their immediate safety, but the very act of attending the session could potentially be triggering, putting their nervous system into a state of activation. When this occurs, and the sympathetic nervous system is activated in the absence of the moderating ventral vagal circuit, the part of the brain that governs rational decision making (the prefrontal cortex) goes offline, which makes it very difficult for your clients to use their words. However, a gentle shift can occur by choosing a practice that is simple, calm, and soothing. Generally, a practice that involves some sort of simple movement can help dissipate some of the excess energy elicited by sympathetic nervous system activation. If you use your knowledge of the polyvagal theory and apply it here alongside a practice from your toolbox, the shift is often immediate, or at least within a few minutes.

For example, you can invite your client to breathe with you and perhaps add some gentle arm movements. **Gentle movement and breathing can help clients tune in to the body and build their capacity to tolerate the reality of what has happened in the past.** I call it making friends with your body, which means rebuilding trust—as you would in any relationship—with yourself and learning to identify and tolerate (perhaps even enjoy) the present-moment experience of one's body. The idea of treating and cultivating one's body as a friend and not an enemy can be tricky to navigate when one has a trauma history, but it's well worth the investment of time and compassion. As Bessel van der Kolk states, "the only way we can change the way we feel is by becoming aware of our inner experience and learning to befriend what is going on inside ourselves" (2014, p. 97).

In my yoga classes, I help clients shift into this befriending ventral vagal state by encouraging students to soften the muscles in their face, such as the jaw and the eyes, and to release any tension they notice in their head, neck, and shoulders. All the while, I remind them to breathe comfortably and fully, as opposed to tightening their muscles and holding their breath, or not being aware of the breath at all. These practices trigger a felt sense of safety, emotional vulnerability, and connection in the body because they activate the vagal brake, which slows down heart rate and reduces sympathetic nervous system activation.

From a practical standpoint, though, it is important to help clients learn and familiarize themselves with these calming practices *ahead of time*. While it is not impossible to teach a client breathing or gentle movement exercises when they are in a state of mobilization, doing so beforehand can allow them to develop muscle memory of the movement. By inviting clients to regularly check in and identify the specific body parts where they may habitually hold tension (such as the jaw, neck, and shoulders), they can activate the social engagement system and anchor themselves in a ventral vagal state most of the time. They can also learn how to recognize the early warning signs in their alarm system so they can identify potential triggers and learn how to manage them.

In addition, as therapists, we know that looking, listening, and speaking—and particularly the *way* we speak—are primary to the efficacy of our therapeutic work. These factors impact our ability to harness the power of co-regulation in the therapy session. **By maintaining a calm, centered presence, you facilitate co-regulation with your client and allow them to return to a calm state as well.** To do so, ensure that you are in a ventral vagal state yourself, and then use a warm, welcoming voice and a soothing tone, and engage with a genuine smile. This is co-regulation in action.

In my role as the executive director of Yoga in Schools, a non-profit organization that trains teachers, parents, and students to nurture their own well-being through yoga, I have often taught teachers and principals to regulate their own nervous system through simple breathing exercises and gentle movements so they can help their students co-regulate. I suggest that they start the day with movement or intersperse movement and breathing throughout the day, particularly during transitional periods (e.g., after lunch) or at other identified problem spots throughout the day. An elementary principal once confronted me in a professional development workshop and said, "So you are suggesting that I just tell Johnny to breathe when he has the chair raised and ready to throw it at me?" I suggested she take cover so she didn't get hurt. The point is, however, that Johnny didn't just *go off*. There were any number of signs along the path to escalation that could have led to an intervention in the form of a kind, soothing conversation to help Johnny make his way back to a ventral vagal state. But this type of co-regulation is only possible if teachers regulate their own nervous systems first. When you are in a ventral vagal state yourself, you are in a state to have others join you.

I have witnessed this shift myself when walking into a room of disabled veterans or an acute care psychiatric facility to facilitate a therapeutic group. I make it a priority to have adequately prepared myself to be there by getting a good night's rest, eating well, staying hydrated, going to the bathroom beforehand, and giving myself some quiet time. These practices allow me to be firmly anchored in a ventral vagal state as I prepare to teach therapeutic yoga to people who have experienced trauma. We have a responsibility to the people we are working with to do our own work and preparation. You never know who may be in front of you or what kind of trauma they may have experienced. And the truth is, they may not be aware of their trauma either.

PART TWO

The Practices

CHAPTER 5

THE SETUP

Beginning anything can seem daunting. Start by making an appointment with yourself and putting yourself on your schedule. Then turn off your cell phone so you won't be interrupted. Treat the time as if it were time with a client—with that client being you. Now you are ready to pick one tool and practice it. Read the script out loud. Move your body, or take the breath as described. When you have the mechanics of it down, take the next step by teaching it to someone else. Start sharing in a low-stakes way, rather than with a client. Practice with your significant other, your kid, or a friend. Pets are fine too, or even an empty chair, but someone who can give you real-time feedback is better.

The point is, we all have to begin somewhere. You won't master, or benefit as much from, utilizing a practice if you haven't tried it many times for yourself. Although your experience with the practice won't necessarily be your client's experience, how the practice feels in your body is very good information for you to have. How did it feel as you were doing it? Did you like it? Was it hard for you to do? It is worth stating that something that is hard for you may be easy for someone else. And something that is easy for you may be hard for someone else. Perhaps, yet again, I'm stating the obvious. But because I have seen such a variety of responses in every group I teach, I don't think I can say it enough. Consider taking some notes or making journal entries for a few minutes after you try each practice. Did anything stand out? How did it feel in the five to ten minutes following? Any information that comes forth will be helpful to you as you move forward.

Remember that any practice can affect you (or your clients) in a different way than is described here. As I mentioned earlier, just because a breathing practice is calming for you and your nervous system, it does not necessarily mean it will be calming for your client. Therefore, I recommend that you experiment with these practices yourself *before* using them with a client. Noticing the effects of a given practice on your own nervous system is the first step to understanding and teaching the practice to someone else and is key to understanding variations in responses to breathing practices. Self-knowledge is needed to contextualize the practices.

Based on my own years of experience, I have tried to anticipate some things you may experience from doing and teaching each practice. Please trust that given the small dosages of practice I am suggesting, the worst that can happen is that you might mix up an inhale with an exhale, or you might hold your breath when you really should not. This is not the end of the world. It just means you need to practice more. When I want to introduce a new practice to a client (and the practice is fairly new to me), I find it helpful to explain my own experience with the practice, followed by, "It may be different for you. Shall we find out?" Then try it out and see what happens.

With your increased self-awareness based upon your prior preparation with the practice, you will know which practices to use and when to offer them. Moreover, just like when you first try most other new experiences, your practice will feel a little awkward and mechanical in the beginning. If you feel this way, you are right on track. Remind yourself what it was like when you first learned a skill that you are now proficient in. I often tell people about my dubious start when I was learning to drive a stick-shift car in Australia. It was terrifying. Why anyone got in the car with me can only be explained as an act of true courage and public service (and eventual public safety).

On the other hand, perhaps you will naturally gravitate toward these practices. If so, good for you. Let this book be a reminder of the value of what you are already doing as a therapist and why it is so important—and then keep practicing. We always get better at things we practice.

THE PRACTICES

While I have included forty-seven separate practices in this book, if you use and master five of them, then I consider my effort of writing this book worthwhile. You don't need to use all of the practices to see results. Use the ones that resonate with you—at least at first. Over time, your repertoire and comfort level will expand. Each practice can stand alone or be combined with other practices. It depends on the time you want to devote to them in the context of the counseling session. I suggest introducing one or two at a time, particularly if you (or your client or group) are new to the idea of including movement and breathing exercises in your therapy sessions.

The practices are divided into four categories to help you discern which practice to use at any given time: **calming practices, balancing practices, energizing practices, and visualizations and meditations.** These are not hard and fast categories but simply generalizations to help you get started. Most practices can be done while seated, and a handful can be done while standing. As you try the practices for yourself and note your own reaction, you will be better prepared to lead and come alongside your clients to help them notice how each practice resonates with them. Of course, their experience with a practice may be similar to, or different from, yours. Also remember that some practices may have more than one effect.

Each practice has a short description and an explanation of why you might use it, what you need to do to prepare yourself and your space, and then the exact script of how I typically teach the practice. Although I include a description of what you might expect to experience from each practice, remember that one size does not fit all. Therefore, it will be up to you as a trained clinician to observe and interpret what you are seeing. I also list a "caution" notice for a handful of the practices to indicate when a certain practice is not appropriate. Please note them. Even if a practice does not have a cautionary warning, it is always okay to decide *not* to do that practice because it doesn't feel right to you (or your client) that day. For any reason. This decision-making process will help retrain the trust between you and your body and allows for potential exploration of a practice in the future.

Each description also states the amount of time that practice may take. Most of the practices will take a little longer at first, though they can become shorter in duration as you gain familiarity with the practice. Conversely, as you become more comfortable with a particular practice, you may want to take more time with it as the situation seems appropriate. Please feel free to do that as well. Make it your own based on what you see and feel. Eventually, including these practices in your sessions will become second nature.

The scripts are formatted so you can simply read them if you wish to. I have included a generous amount of ellipses to remind you to slow your reading voice. A new paragraph signifies a longer pause, or silence. The italicized words are directives (highlighted in gray) for you that are not intended to be read out loud. Use a calm, steady voice when leading the practices. Slow the pace. Your tendency when reading the script will likely be to read too fast. Take your time. The more you practice speaking, the less likely it is that you will add filler words like *um*. Adjust the volume of your voice so you can be easily heard. Use a pleasant, conversational tone. Say it like you mean it.

In my early days of teaching (and even now), I made an audio recording of myself practice teaching so I could evaluate myself. Of course, if you want to record yourself in an actual session you will need your client's permission, and it would not be appropriate to do in certain settings. The recordings are strictly for my own learning and self-evaluation. Make sure you follow the standard ethical guidelines that your licensure requires.

TRANSITIONING IN AND OUT OF A PRACTICE

Each practice gives a suggested point in session when it might be useful to introduce the practice. You will notice that most practices begin and end with "Notice how you are feeling in this moment" and a call to tune in to present-moment reality. As you start using the vocabulary of cultivating mindfulness, there will be some natural pauses and moments of silence that arise, which will allow time for the important *noticing* aspect of the practice. These pauses will naturally slow down the session and allow the client's agenda to unfold more organically. This slowing down also will allow you to offer choices, such as "I have been trying out some new self-care practices in the form of specific breathing practices. I am wondering if you would like to try this short centering exercise to see how it feels to you?"

In addition, it is good to take a few moments to set up a ritual that signifies the beginning of a session and that invites you and your client into the present moment. I recently completed a training to be a spiritual director, and I have started offering clients several ways to begin our sessions together. That may include a time of silence, silence and a prayer (with words), or a short standing or sitting movement practice (usually five to seven minutes) to help them (and me) center and ground. I tend to keep it simple and keep the use of technology to a minimum. You can also consider lighting a candle, sounding a chime, or taking a few deep breaths together. If fire codes prevent you from using an open flame, consider using battery-powered candles. I have used them often to great effect.

Clients usually know what they need, and they appreciate that they may be better able to share what is on their mind after engaging in one or more of these practices first. You may also find that offering one of these short practices at the start of your session will facilitate your counseling goals with your client. By the way, it is okay (highly recommended, actually) to experiment until you find a rhythm that works for you.

Finally, for a more complete sense of closure after any of the practices, you may want to cue clients to direct their awareness to their internal sensations. This action grounds the practice while building interoceptive awareness. There are many ways to do this. The following are some sample scripts from the LifeForce Yoga Teacher Training Protocol:

- Notice your right hand... notice your left hand... notice your right foot... notice your left foot... notice your whole body.

- Sense into your right hand... sense into your left hand... sense into your right foot... sense into your left foot... notice your whole body.

- Say to yourself, either silently or quietly, "I am" on the inhale and "here" on the exhale.

In several of the practices, the cueing to direct awareness is included in the script already. However, this type of cueing could be added to any of the practices.

Cassandra's Story: The Power of Rituals

Cassandra is an analytical and intuitive therapist who, several years into her thriving (faith-based) private practice, was seeing more and more clients with trauma. It became clear to her that she needed to dive deeper into bottom-up practices, like movement and breath work, to better attune to her clients and to better assist them in accessing their inner resources. Always wanting to continue growing as a therapist herself, Cassandra had read Bessel van der Kolk's *The Body Keeps the Score* and was deeply moved by his work. By the time she received an invitation to try my new training, Chair Yoga for *Clinicians*, she already was intrigued and ready to learn more.

The training was divided into two four-hour sessions. What Cassandra appreciated the most was not only learning about the science behind the tools but taking the time to practice them. She understood that her body needed to learn the practices first so she could use them authentically in a session. The training also focused on small group interactions where Cassandra had to teach some practices to her colleagues. She found this style of learning most useful in consolidating her own understanding of how the practices felt in her own body.

Like most professional development courses that Cassandra was excited about, she committed to practicing right away and tried out some of the practices with certain clients. She was amazed at what she felt and saw the very first week she tried them. She began to gain more confidence in determining what practice to use and when to use it. She remembers very vividly when she introduced a breathing meditation to a client named Sandy. Sandy arrived late to the session and slumped into her seat with a heightened sense of self-flagellation in her demeanor. In the past, this was followed by many words describing this torturous state of being. On this occasion, Cassandra stopped her before any words came out and asked if they could try something together. Sandy agreed. The breath meditation lasted for five minutes. Cassandra could see and feel something was shifting internally for Sandy. She then chose to use a powerful image, an ancient icon called *The Trinity*, for her and Sandy to sit with and take in. Sandy soon asked to begin every session with a breath meditation. Cassandra credits this particular practice and session as a pivotal one that shifted Sandy out of her head and into her body, out of reactivity and into receptivity, out of condemning isolation and into compassionate community.

PERSONAL AGENCY AND AWARENESS

When offering the practices to your clients, make sure to emphasize their choice in deciding whether they want to participate. The practice of self-selecting whether to do, or not to do, something is very powerful. I recall an experience I had while teaching at Shuman Juvenile Detention Center about ten years ago. I was allowed access to the locked unit to teach a yoga class. The young men gathered around, and I explained who I was and what we would be doing. I continued by inviting them to participate as I was setting up the room. A resident came up to me and said, "Hey, Ms. Yoga, do I have to do it or not?" I replied,

No, but you might want to consider trying. Perhaps there will be something in this class just for you. This class is about moving your body and breathing to find some inner peace. I've never been able to force anyone to breathe or move, and I'm not about to start now. You in?

The young man looked at me as if I didn't know we were in a locked facility and said, "Are you telling me I don't have to do this if I don't want to? Cause I ain't never done yoga before." It was true that, with regard to virtually all other aspects of his life inside the center, he had to do what he was told, and he was no longer making decisions for himself about many aspects of his life. Part of my job, perhaps even before either of us understood the implications, was to help him reconnect with the part of himself that made decisions and to support his capacity to do so, even regarding seemingly small things like moving his body and breathing in a certain way.

Of course, I passionately wanted each resident to try yoga, but I knew the importance of allowing them to make their own choice to participate. Ultimately, he did join in the class that day, and we both could recognize that it was his choice to do so. Just to be clear, the alternatives were not terribly interesting. He could quietly do homework or read a book, but he could not go to his room or watch television. To me, this incident brought home the point that the power of deciding not to do a practice can be equally as important as trying a practice. So, listen carefully to what your clients are telling you and make sure they know they can opt out of a practice at *any time* for *any reason*.

Feeling the Resistance

I vividly remember a day when I showed up to teach class at the detention center and everybody on the unit participated. At first, I was delighted. But after a few minutes, something felt off to me, and I couldn't figure out what it was. About twenty minutes into the sixty-minute class, I decided to test *my hunch*—the tension felt almost unbearable. I paused the class and simply said, "Did something happen before class?" Crickets. I waited. Finally, one of the staff admitted that the morning had not gone so well. As "punishment," this staff member had told everyone that they had to participate in class whether they wanted to or not. This news made me very upset, but I knew better than to get into a power struggle with a staff member in front of the residents.

In the moment, it felt like my only option was to stop the class and acknowledge the resistance. I did not feel confident enough in my skills at that time to do that. Instead, I merely ignored the information and carried on with the class. Nothing changed except now I knew that the resistance I felt was real. My body felt it even though my intellect couldn't explain it. I doubt anyone reaped much benefit from the class other than a time-filler. This was not a satisfying experience in any way. However, I was later able to reflect on what happened, and it informed my check-in process with the staff and the need to emphasize choice and personal agency. Exercising power over others was counterproductive.

In addition, trust that when you give clients an option to try something different—such as moving in a session when that is not what you usually do—and they say yes or give you a head nod, that they will follow your lead. They always have the option of saying no or choosing another tool. And with some regular training, they will become familiar with enough tools to pick a starting point. **Trust that they are the experts on themselves and their own experience.**

To help clients develop a level of awareness regarding the practices that may best suit them in a particular movement, I have discovered that using the image of a toolbelt is helpful. This

Calming	Balancing	Energizing
Peaceful	Integrating	Mobilizing
Serene	Stabilizing	Activating
Quieting	Collected	Stimulating
Focusing	Connected	Motivating
Soothing	Content	Elevating

Figure 4. The Toolbelt

imaginary toolbelt has three pockets. The pocket on the left is for calming practices, the one on the right is for energizing practices, and the one in the middle is for balancing practices—practices that I find both calming and energizing at the same time. There are multiple words that can be substituted for *calming*, *balancing*, and *energizing*. See Figure 4 for some other examples of words you can use in your toolbelt image. Remember, these are flexible categories, not ones that are hard and fast.

Another way to help clients understand which practice is best for them in the moment—in addition to simply experimenting with a practice—is to use the movement of energy scale (see Figure 5). This is a visual prop I created several years ago. It is a concrete way to demonstrate the movement of energy by using a number continuum. Here, I deliberately use the words *anxiety* and *depression* to illustrate the general concept that depression is associated with too little energy and anxiety with too much energy. Whether or not someone has a diagnosis of clinical depression or anxiety is not the point here. The point is to gain an understanding that all of us are moving back and forth on the continuum all day long in some way or another. Everything we do and don't do—from breathing, moving, eating, drinking, working, resting, and socializing—moves us one way or the other on the scale. This realization can be useful in developing self-knowledge and awareness. We are not machines; we are humans with very real limitations.

While this fact may seem a bit discouraging, I have found it quite liberating to understand my limits and to stop acting like Superwoman. My body, like most bodies, needs a certain amount of sleep and water (among other things) to function. For example, knowing that I need nine hours of sleep to function well, and that I must drink at least sixty-four ounces of water per day, makes those actions a priority for me. Meeting these needs has accumulated benefits for me.

The goal is to land somewhere between 4 and 6 as an optimal operating range. Knowing where you are on the continuum is very helpful in identifying which practice may be beneficial in a particular moment. Start by picking any practice, doing it several times over, noticing the effect, and then asking yourself, "Do I move toward more energy or less energy?" Then put the practice in one of the three pockets on your imaginary toolbelt.

Both the toolbelt and movement of energy scale highlight the importance of ensuring that you and your clients learn which practice to use at any given time. I find that teaching my clients *how* to decide on a practice, and when to do it, reminds them that they have choice or personal agency, which is often easy to forget when they are in the midst of experiencing the effects of trauma.

Energy: Too Much or Too Little?		
Low	Optimal	High
1	5	10
Depression		Anxiety

Figure 5. Movement of Energy Scale

YOUR LEARNING PROCESS

It may not be obvious from my writing that I spent twenty years in Australia. As a result, I have an accent, even after thirty years of living in the U.S. Even now, when I teach or even say "Hello," someone looks at me quizzically. I have learned to use the unusual gift of an accent as a superpower to draw people into the practice, but I nearly always explain myself and say, "It is very important to me that you understand what I am talking about." And it is. But there are times that my accent or a turn-of-phrase may create confusion. Therefore, I give people multiple invitations, opportunities, and permission to ask for clarification. Make sure that you do too (wherever you are from).

How you see people responding to the instruction you give will also be helpful feedback. Always observe and monitor your client's response. I always ask myself, "Are people doing what I just asked or instructed them to do?" If they're not, most of the time I have found that it's because I delivered the instruction in a way that wasn't clear, not because of their lack of comprehension. I must take full ownership of my words and find another way to explain myself.

As the teacher and therapist, I need to adapt my teaching style to the learning style of the person in front of me and not the other way around. Some people will need to see a handout with a written explanation. If so, you can have that ready to give them. Others will be distracted by written words and need clear, precise verbal cues instead. Others will need you to demonstrate the action and then do it with them. I do a combination of all three, though I generally don't give a handout until the end of class (if I am using one at all) because I don't want people jumping back into their "thinking" brain. Sometimes I will say, "Let's get out of our heads and into our bodies" and then begin moving, even if it is a simple action of inhaling the hands into the air and exhaling them back down again.

Teaching clients to connect to the feeling and sensation of movement will also help them connect to the feeling and sensation of their emotions. We build our capacity to feel similar to how we build muscle: a little at a time. Therefore, start with concrete actions (like the sensation of moving one's arms skyward) and then gently progress to the less concrete (like asking clients where they might feel gratitude in their body).

Normalizing and naming each person's unique learning process can be powerful. Often, clients will ask me questions like, "How should this feel?" and "Am I doing it right?" What I am trying to teach them is to instead ask themselves, "How does it feel *to me*?" Since everyone is different, each client will experience the practices differently. Nevertheless, you still can make some general points about each of the practices, which are noted at the beginning of each practice. But if you don't highlight the fact that diverse experiences are normal, then you'll get tiring and mistaken responses, like "I am not good at yoga because I felt it here (when you said I should feel it there)" or "I didn't notice anything." The point is if you do some practice each day, you can't *not* be good at yoga. You could *not* practice, but that is different.

Practicing is everything. I am going to say it again, just to be sure it sinks in. Practicing is everything. Practice on yourself. An ancient yogic text says it like this: "Practice becomes firmly grounded when well attended to for a long time without break and in all earnestness" (Satchidananda, 1985, p. 6). Link your breath and movement and move only in your pain-free range of motion—the first two foundational principles. Take note of what happens over time. Try it for five minutes daily over the course of a week.

Although some research has shown that frequent practice of short duration is of greatest benefit (Ross, Friedmann, Bevans, & Thomas, 2012), the dosage response in yoga is not yet properly understood, meaning that the amount of yoga needed to create a therapeutic response has not been systematically studied enough to know the answer (Cook-Cottone, 2013). Until that time, what we *do* know is that habits drive behavior. Repeating the same action over time creates new neural pathways in the brain through a process called neuroplasticity.

So by all means, keep going to a weekly yoga class that you love and that is part of your self-care routine. It can only help. And at the same time, remember that yoga's effectiveness seems to come from small amounts of *daily* practice over time. There is no such thing as "one and done" in yoga. We do it repeatedly, eventually cultivating five to thirty minutes of daily practice. If five minutes per day is what you can do successfully, then do that. My own practice each day ranges from ten to sixty minutes, depending on my schedule.

SPATIAL AWARENESS

Simple movement is an effective way to help someone get connected to their body. That said, there will be times when your client will do something different than what you had in mind, even when you think you gave clear instruction and simple demonstrations. If they heard you and saw you demonstrate a practice—yet what they are doing is nothing like what you intended—then rather than perceiving what they are doing as right or wrong, I prefer to perceive (and receive) their interpretation as information I can use to improve the effectiveness of treatment in the future.

If you work from the premise that everyone is doing the best they can with their currently available resources, you have important information about the extent to which that client's nervous system is integrated or not integrated. For example, their ability to know where their body is in space—proprioception—may be off. I have observed over many years that people with PTSD often have a reduced capacity to notice where their body begins and ends, even if they consider themselves to be well-coordinated and spatially oriented. This lapse in spatial awareness can be an obstacle physically and mentally. It may even be a source of embarrassment.

Therefore, even though many people naturally tend to close their eyes when we start to move or breathe, there are times when I will encourage someone to open their eyes and look at me during an exercise (though the choice to keep their eyes open or closed is always theirs). I do this for a few reasons: **(1)** I want to be sure they are still with me in the present moment, and it is usually easier to be present with your eyes open; **(2)** I want them to use their sense of sight to orient themselves to their surroundings, such as the chair they are sitting on, to me, or to other people if we are in a group; and **(3)** I can gently cue them to use the environment. In addition, when a client's eyes are closed, trauma can interrupt the proper functioning of the brain that interprets the present experience (van der Kolk, 2014). By keeping their eyes open and focusing on the sensations of gentle movement, they can reorient to the here and now where they feel present, safe, and accounted for—all good conditions that constitute a good place where therapy can begin.

You can also help clients navigate the space by organizing the environment in a way that doesn't get in the way of someone's bodily movements. For example, if the practice you choose involves moving the arms in some way, be sure there is ample space to do so. Practice in the space where you plan to teach so you can get a sense of what could get in the way of someone's bodily movements. This may require rearranging your office furniture, knickknacks, and lamps so they don't become hazardous with a casual arm movement. Exaggerate the movements just to be sure a plant or wall accessory is not in harm's way. You may also need to provide extra cues to remind someone where their body begins and ends, as proprioception improves with practice.

If you are teaching in a group, remind clients to navigate the space with their neighbors. I find that mentioning spatial awareness—even with a little levity, such as "Try not to scratch your neighbor's nose"—is enough of a cue to help people mindfully navigate their space. If they are still unable to refrain from bumping into someone else, this gives you some helpful information about both the state of their awareness and their ability to be oriented in the space.

In addition to rearranging the space in a way that facilitates bodily movement, consider how you can maximize other elements of the atmosphere. For example, harsh florescent lighting can be problematic for some people. Dim the lights if you can, or perhaps use floor or table lamps for more diffused lighting. Consider natural light if your office has windows. I take my own practice outside whenever possible.

OBSERVATION

Part of your job is to observe what is going on with your clients, so when you invite someone to close their eyes and they choose to do so, you need to keep your eyes open. This level of attentiveness is particularly important if you are teaching a group. As you observe your clients during the practices, pay attention to signs of tension they may be exhibiting. If you observe tension in your client's face as they move, a gentle reminder to soften the jaw or relax the face will help them bring awareness to this tension. If you have trouble seeing tension in another's body, it does get easier over time. A fun practice is to sit in front of a mirror and tense different body parts just to get used to seeing what it looks like.

In addition, observation is about noticing the breath. Throughout the practices, you will see that I use the phrases "notice your breathing" or "notice your breath" very often. Sometimes I vary the script by mentioning specific characteristics to notice about the breath that you may not have thought about before, such as:

- Notice the texture of the breath.
- Notice the length of the breath.
- Is the breath shallow or deep?
- Where do you feel the breath in your body?
- Is it a short breath or a long breath?
- Feel the coolness of the breath as you inhale.
- Feel the warmth of the breath as you exhale.

And then again, it may simply be hard to notice anything about breathing at all. You may also notice in the scripts that I don't say, "Take a deep breath." Although the goal is to eventually (and hopefully) take many deep breaths, the practices in this book are about the multiple small steps that can be taken along the path to finding and enjoying a longer, fuller breath.

When you become more practiced at noticing your breath, it will feel more natural to notice the different characteristics of the breath, and it may even become a source of endless fascination. To practice noticing, begin paying attention to those around you. How are they breathing? What do you notice about their breathing? Can you hear someone near you breathing? Once you start noticing such things, it is hard to not notice. Noticing the breath can become your superpower.

Any time you or a client tries something new, particularly a new breathing pattern or bodily movement, it is possible the body may respond with slight dizziness or nausea. This is common, so be on the lookout for this possibility as part of your observation. If this happens, sit if you are standing, and breathe normally—whatever that means for you. The feeling should pass within a minute or two. If it doesn't, then this practice may not be for you. In addition, the more you practice, the less likely it is that you will experience the dizziness and nausea. Listen to the wisdom of your body.

If you are in the middle of a session and notice that your client is looking increasingly anxious, you may want to pause the session and say, "I am noticing there are some emotions arising for you. I am wondering where you might be on the movement of energy scale?" If your client acknowledges that they are moving into an anxious state, you could then inquire if they would like to try a short exercise to see if they can return somewhere closer to the middle of the scale. If they agree and feel calmer following the exercise, it is good to point out that they were able to soothe themselves and follow up with a question such as, "Are there other times it might be helpful to soothe yourself in this way?" Yes, it is a leading question, but their answer helps them to connect the dots themselves.

Alternatively, you can redirect them back to their imaginary toolbelt by asking, "In which pocket of your toolbelt does this practice belong?" If they really don't know yet, it is usually because they simply need more experience with the practice to identify (with some level of certainty) how the practice affects them.

SOME ADDITIONAL TOOLS

To enhance delivery of the practices, you might consider incorporating some of the following additional tools into your sessions:

- **Folding chairs:** If you have couches or armchairs in your office, you may want to invest in a few metal folding chairs to have ready for a seated practice. While not essential, this type of chair will be more comfortable and practical for the type of practices described here.
- **Chime:** It is simple, soothing, and can be easily purchased at many types of stores or online.
- **Music:** I use an iPod Classic so I don't need to have my phone visible. It also doesn't require wireless internet to play music. I am rarely able to access the Internet (in any form) in many of the facilities I teach—hence the need for lower-tech options. I also use a speaker with good sound quality, with either an audio cable or Bluetooth capabilities. Old school CD players are just fine too. If you plan on using just one track, have it cued and ready.

If you plan to play music from your phone, include it on a playlist and put your phone in airplane mode so incoming calls don't interrupt your session. If you plan on using your streaming music service, make sure that it will work in the location where you intend to use it. Whatever format of music you choose, be familiar with your equipment so you don't fumble with it.

As you develop familiarity with these practices and lead your clients through each exercise, remember that your job is to be in a ventral vagal state: calm and alert, yet relaxed and focused.

CHAPTER 6

CALMING PRACTICES

The ability to calm and soothe oneself, or to simply find one's place of serenity, is an increasingly important skill to have in times of uncertainty. Slowing one's breathing has long been recognized as a way to calm down because it stimulates the vagus nerve, which in turn increases parasympathetic nervous system activity—the body's "brake." Intuitively, our breathing slows down when we find equanimity, but even when it doesn't, we can notice, cultivate, and train our capacity to do so. The breath is the most direct access we have to influence the nervous system.

While many of the following practices are focused on the breath, others include gentle movement. Sometimes we need to add movement simply to dissipate the buildup of nervous energy that we all experience from time to time.

PRACTICE 1
CHAIR MOUNTAIN

Time: 1-2 minutes

Description: Chair Mountain is a pose you should practice daily, or anytime you find yourself in a chair, because its benefits are so profound and far reaching. Daily practice will allow you to experience these benefits. Like Mountain Pose, which is the most foundational of yoga poses, Chair Mountain requires more from us than initially meets the (inner) eye. When done attentively, Chair Mountain helps you maintain good posture and supports good biomechanics, whether you are at your desk or behind your steering wheel. At the same time, sitting for hours on end will tax your body no matter how good your posture is. The spinal load is greater while sitting than standing. Alternating between sitting and standing throughout your day, if possible, is a good way to support or heal the spine.

Special Preparation: A kitchen chair or a metal folding chair is best for this practice. It is fine to use the back of the chair for support, but over time, you and your back will not need the constant support of the chair. Your abdominal muscles and quadriceps will help support the spine.

Script

Sit straight in your chair… feet hip-width apart… scoot forward on your chair so there is a space between your back and the back of the chair… the support of the chair is always there when you need it.

Move your belly button toward your spine to engage the abdominal muscles… let your muscles do the work, not your breath… see if you can let the breath be smooth and flowing while maintaining this slight engagement.

Press your feet into the floor and pretend that you are slowly straightening your spine. Notice if you can engage your quads (the muscles on the front of your thighs)… place your hands on your quads so you can feel when your quads are engaging… the muscles will feel harder… if your back needs a rest… it is always okay to use the back of your chair to support your spine.

Notice the effort of sitting upright… now relax and soften everything…. good, observe the difference. Now engage the quads again… soften the face… breathe… and relax.

Your homework is to practice Chair Mountain for a few minutes each day until it becomes effortless and comfortable.

PRACTICE 2
RESTING

Time: 4-5 minutes

Description: It is important to distinguish between *rest* and *sleep* here. When we intentionally take time to rest, we evoke the relaxation response as we slow down the breath and minimize movement. Rest gives our bodies a break, which can, in turn, lead to good sleep. Although I have struggled with rest my whole life—mostly because of fear of missing out (FOMO)—we all have to face the limits of our humanity at some point. In fact, learning to rest in small increments can help us face and perhaps expand those limits. Resting can help us cultivate a more loving sense of self as we find refreshment from downtime and even develop a tolerance for it.

Taking time to regularly prioritize downtime may seem a little countercultural, especially when most of us try to cram too much into each day. But what would our life look like if we resisted the "doing too much" urge, paced ourselves a little more, rested, and reflected more often? Perhaps we would accomplish a surprising amount, but that's not really what I am making a case for here. Instead, I am talking about *doing less*. The benefits of even ten minutes of rest can be amazingly revelatory and refreshing—if you can get over the little voice in your head that says, "Why bother?"

Resting is part of *every* yoga class I have ever taken or taught over the last twenty years. The Sanskrit word for this part of class is called *savasana*, which means Corpse Pose (and this is a pretty good description for what it looks like too). Traditionally and most often, the pose is done lying down. However, I have taken the essence of the intention of *savasana* and given you a seated variation. It is wonderful to try out this practice while lying on the floor, but if that is not physically possible, either due to practical limitations you are experiencing in your body or not having enough space, sitting in a chair is a good substitute.

The goal is to do nothing. At all. That is why it is so easy… and so hard. The practice is about your comfort. It is about letting go, which includes letting go of tension from your body and thoughts or patterns of thinking that no longer serve you. It is not even about breathing a certain way. Just breathing in any way that is comfortable for you will suffice. When I slow down, I have found that some emotions may arise that I have not given myself time to feel. Sometimes tears appear. Try to welcome what arises. Notice any feelings that arise. Naming your feelings can be helpful to validate and give expression to something that is already there.

My challenge for you is to try it. Practice resting as if your life depends on it. Try ten minutes a day for a month, and just see what happens. This practice is usually done at the end of a class, but you could use it any time during a session to simply practice resting and resetting.

Special Preparation: If you are going to do this practice lying down, you might like to use a yoga mat. I also like to use yoga blocks or a bolster (or a rolled-up blanket or towel) under my knees. Additionally, an eye mask or eye pillow—something with a little weight over the eyes—is usually very relaxing. However, all these props can be dispensed with. Sitting comfortably in a chair with your back straight and supported can become restful as well.

Script

Let's take five minutes to rest. It will help integrate the experience
of your yoga practice (or therapy) into your nervous system. There
is no goal… the idea is to do nothing… which can be
surprisingly hard for some of us.

Lying Down Variation:

Gather your props (if you have them) to make yourself
comfortable. Take your time. It is worth the effort.

Now lie down, cover yourself up, make any necessary
adjustments to your set-up so you are as comfortable as possible,
and settle in. The idea is to be still in the body and still in the mind.

Remember there is nothing to do… nowhere to go… no particular
way to breathe… just let yourself be… you are exactly where you need to
be… right here… right now.

Inhale love… exhale peace… inhale love… exhale peace.

If you find yourself thinking, just notice that you are thinking.
Don't judge the thought, and come gently back to your breath.
Repeat this process of thinking, noticing, not judging, and
returning to your breath as many times as you need to.

I will watch the time… don't worry if you nod off… resting is
different from napping… though at first it may feel the same…
but eventually… with practice… you will be relaxed in your body
and alert in your mind… it is a beautiful space to be in.

> ***Keep time for four minutes.***

Start to wiggle your fingers… wiggle your toes… move
your body in a way that feels comforting and nourishing… perhaps
hugging your knees to your chest… perhaps stretching out your arms…
taking all the time you need, gradually come back to sitting… notice
how you are feeling in this moment.

Seated Variation:

Sit comfortably in your chair, using the back of the chair to
support your spine… your feet are on the floor… feel free to
close your eyes… or simply soften your gaze a little.

Remember there is nothing to do… nowhere to go… no
particular way to breathe… just let yourself be… you are
exactly where you need to be… right here… right now.

Inhale love… exhale peace… inhale love… exhale peace.

If you find yourself thinking, just notice that you are thinking.
Don't judge the thought, and come gently back to your breath.
Repeat this process of thinking, noticing, not judging, and
returning to your breath as many times as you need to.

I will watch the time… don't worry if you nod off… resting
is different from napping… though at first it may feel the same… but
eventually… with practice… you will be relaxed in your body and
alert in your mind… it is a beautiful space to be in.

Keep time for four minutes.

Start to wiggle your fingers… wiggle your toes… move your body in a
way that feels comforting and nourishing… perhaps stretching out
your arms… taking all the time you need, gradually orient yourself to
the room… notice how you are feeling in this moment.

PRACTICE 3
CENTERING

Time: 2-3 minutes

Description: You can complete this short centering practice at the start of the session, as soon as you and your client are both seated, or you can use it at any other point in session if either one of you needs re-centering for any reason. Centering prepares you to listen and will establish a safe container for therapy to begin. It is likely that your clients will expect you to take the lead regarding how to begin. They will take their cues from you—literally. Make sure to sit as you would like them to sit: straight and tall, but not rigid, and with the breath flowing easily. This posture is important to activate mirror neurons. Mirror neurons help us to learn by imitation and reflect an action we see another doing.

Special Preparation: Sit on a chair or firm couch to support your posture, given that it is difficult to sit straight and tall on a couch that is soft and cushy. Complete whatever ritual you usually do to signal the beginning of the session, such as lighting a candle.

Script

I'd like to begin by focusing on centering our attention
in the present moment. Feel free to have your eyes
open or closed, whichever way feels better to you.

Feel your feet on the floor... notice your bottom on the
chair... feel the support of the floor and the chair under your
body... notice your breath... no need to make any changes.
Just notice that you are breathing.

Are you breathing through your nose?... are you breathing
through your mouth?... are you breathing slowly or quickly?

There are no right or wrong answers here, just observations
for you to make.

If you feel like it, and if you are not already
breathing through your nose, try it.

Notice the pace of your breathing... start by counting
the length of your inhale and then your exhale... don't change it;
just notice what it is.

Does it seem irregular?... or is there a pattern emerging?... remember, there are no right or wrong answers. You simply are gathering information for yourself... for example, if you are inhaling and exhaling for a count of three, let's try inhaling and exhaling for a count of four—or something similar—or feel free to keep breathing as you are and simply notice that you are inhaling and exhaling.

Inhale... exhale... inhale... exhale. Notice that you are here now... present with your breath... bring your attention back to your feet... now to your belly... now to your heart... now to your head... inhale and exhale.

If your eyes are closed, open them slowly and orient yourself to the room... notice how you are feeling in this moment.

If you would like to do so, consider sharing a word or phrase to describe how you are feeling right now.

PRACTICE 4

GROUNDING

Time: 2-10 minutes

Description: There are times when we are anxious or feeling the early stages of being overwhelmed with our thoughts, and we get so caught up in our minds that we lose awareness of the body. Finding a way to physically ground ourselves and reconnect to the body is empowering. It helps us to metaphorically tether ourselves to the present moment. We can do so by drawing attention to the fact that our head and feet are indeed connected by the body. This factual information is literally grounding—*Ah, yes! My head is attached to the rest of my body. My feet are on the ground, and it's all connected*—which can be a very powerful antidote to overwhelming thoughts.

If you notice that your client is having difficulty focusing, then this practice may be a good one with which to start. You can use it as a stand-alone practice or pair it with another practice, such as the various Movements of the Spine (chapter 7, practices 1–3). Encourage your client to keep their eyes open, as it is not necessarily a good idea for them to close their eyes if they are not feeling grounded. Keeping their eyes open will help them remain in the present moment, instead of being distracted with their thoughts, and can increase their sense of safety.

Special Preparation: Grounding is a standing practice, so make sure there is room to swing the arms freely. If you prefer to do this exercise sitting, there is a seated variation that omits the arm movements and body twisting.

Script

Standing Variation:

Let's begin the practice of grounding. Begin by noticing the breath…
no need to make changes… what is the texture of your breath today?…
is it smooth and soft?… or is it rough and raggedy?… or something else?

Take a glance down at your feet. Notice them… notice the
support of the floor under your feet… now bring your
awareness all the way to the crown of your head.

Now pretend that you are drawing an imaginary line from
your head down your center, all the way to your feet.

Look at your feet on the floor again. Lift your
toes if you can… then relax the toes.

Shift your awareness back to the crown of your head… again, focus your awareness to the imaginary line that runs from your head to your feet.

Your head and feet are connected through your body… observe the connection… your feet are on the ground.

Return to observing the sensations of your breath… notice your inhale and your exhale.

Now begin to shape your breath… inhale for a count of three, and sigh it out. Inhale, two, three. Exhale.

Sigh—with your mouth slightly open—making the sigh audible.

Let's try that again. Inhale, two, three, and exhale. Sigh it out. One more time. Inhale, two, three, exhale, sigh it out.

Now let's move the body gently from side to side.

Demonstrate moving the body left to right and right to left, simply shifting your weight from one foot to the other.

Do a slight twist, letting your arms hang by your sides, gently twisting from side to side. Your feet are still and your knees are soft. Your body is leading the movement and your arms are just going along for the ride—as if you are moving empty coat sleeves.

Shake your hands a little… notice how you are feeling… when you are ready, take a seat.

Seated Variation:

Sit up straight in your chair… let's begin the practice of grounding. Begin by noticing the breath… no need to make changes… what is the texture of your breath today?… is it smooth and soft?… or is it rough and raggedy?… or something else?

Take a glance down at your feet. Notice them… notice the support of the floor under your feet… now bring your awareness all the way to the crown of your head.

Now pretend that you are drawing an imaginary line from your head down your center, all the way to your feet.

Look at your feet on the floor again. Lift your toes if you can… then relax the toes.

Shift your awareness back to the crown of your head… again, focus your awareness to the imaginary line that runs from your head to your feet.

Your head and feet are connected through your body…your feet are on the ground.

Return to observing the sensations of your breath… notice your inhale and your exhale.

Now begin to shape your breath… inhale for a count of three, and sigh it out. Inhale, two, three. Exhale.

Sigh—with your mouth slightly open—making the sigh audible.

Let's try that again. Inhale, two, three, and exhale. Sigh it out. One more time. Inhale, two, three, exhale, sigh it out.

Gently shake out your hands… stomp your feet a few times… notice how you are feeling.

PRACTICE 5
NASAL BREATHING

Time: 2-3 minutes

Description: There are many reasons that nasal breathing is a better choice than mouth breathing. But rather than think about a right and wrong way to breathe, I find it more helpful to think that some ways of breathing are more efficient than others. For example, nasal breathing is more efficient in that it allows for a better exchange of carbon dioxide for oxygen. Your nasal hairs also warm, filter, and humidify the air you breathe in. In addition, studies show that people who are nasal breathers have fewer respiratory infections compared to mouth breathers. Therefore, my recommendation is to practice nasal breathing until it is your default breath. The practice is quiet and unobtrusive, so you can do it while waiting in line at the bank, at a traffic light, or while on hold with the utility company. It is a nice and simple place to start.

I have never seen anyone struggle with nasal breathing, unless they were congested, in which case nasal breathing may be out of the question. I have also found that some older adults may have a pattern of open mouth breathing, but it is not particularly hard to retrain this habit if they are open to it.

Special Preparation: Nasal breathing can be done anytime, anywhere. Sitting, standing, or lying down. Keep some tissues handy. It is often good to blow your nose before the practice to clear the airways.

Caution: I can't think of a bad time to try nasal breathing. However, if you have some sort of congestion or a deviated septum, breathe however you need to because nasal breathing may not be accessible.

Script

Let's begin by noticing your breathing as it is... no
changes... no judgments... just breathing.

Notice the temperature of your breath... feel its coolness as you inhale... and
the warmth of your exhale... those are your nasal hairs hard at work warming,
humidifying, and filtering the air you breathe.

Notice what parts of your body are moving... put your hands on the
sides of your rib cage... feel the ribs moving under your hands.

If your mouth is not already closed, then close your mouth, and
inhale and exhale through your nose... good... let's keep going...
see if you can slow your breath down... just a little.

Put your top lip on your bottom lip.

If someone is clearly not breathing through the nose or is struggling, try facing them, pursing your lips, and pointing to your nose while you continue breathing in through your nose and out through your nose.

Let's try it again together... good... let's keep going for another few breaths.

Notice how you feel.

This request will sound strange, but I am going to ask you to practice nasal breathing as your homework. I want you to become better and better at it... I am serious. It will change your life.

PRACTICE 6
VERTICAL ARM RAISES

Time: 2-3 minutes

Description: The simple action of raising the arms on an inhale and lowering them on an exhale is a concrete demonstration of linking breath to movement. I have had many clients really *feel* the power of doing yoga because they were echoing the movement of their breath in their bodies with the movement of their arms. You and your client will have a felt sense of the practice. This exercise can be done anytime, but I often do it at the beginning of a session to kick things off.

Because this action is simple enough for most people to do, you can really see who is alert, present, and able to follow directions. I have also found that this practice is useful in my work with older adults and wheelchair-bound veterans. When I watch where they place their hands, I can learn some information about their range of motion and proprioceptive abilities.

I tend to do this exercise in sets of three, and I may insert it between other movement or breathing exercises as a transitional movement. This repetition allows someone to feel as if they are developing familiarity with yoga. This satisfying feeling of developing mastery usually encourages them to continue with the practice, and it prepares them for more complex movement later in the teaching process.

Script

Remember today that we are only moving in our pain-free range of motion, and we are linking our breath to our movement. First, sit up tall with your feet on the floor, spine straight, chest lifted... good.

Let's inhale the arms toward the ceiling and exhale them down to your sides... the movement is as if you were rolling paint on a wall in front of you... just a bit higher than your head, if that movement is available to you today... let's do that again... good... keep going... find a flow to the movements... and continue.

> *Move your arms up and down slowly, smoothly, and repeatedly, in sync with the breath.*

Simply doing what you can do without pain... whatever that is, is fine... find a pace and a rhythm to your movement... make it graceful... let it be slow... inhale and exhale... this is a good way to heighten your awareness of your breath by linking your breath to your movement.

> **Keep moving your arms up and down.**

Notice how the bones in your arm are moving in your shoulder sockets... is it smooth?... is it jerky?... does it require effort?... do you feel some resistance?... is one arm stronger than the other?... if you feel some resistance, simply pause and breathe. Don't force the movement... inhale, lift... exhale, down... one more time.

Good... now relax your arms at your sides... notice what you feel... notice any changes or awareness of your shoulders.

PRACTICE 7
HORIZONTAL ARM RAISES

Time: 2-3 minutes

Description: This practice is a simple departure from vertical arm raises. It is another way to demonstrate linking the breath to movement in a different plane and is very doable for most people. When people enjoy a positive and successful experience with a practice, they are often motivated to do more. Repetition stimulates the development of new neural pathways and promotes neurogenesis, which is the growth of new brain cells. Because this practice is simple and accessible, I often introduce it earlier in a session, but it can be done anytime. If your client is generally a physically inactive person and is quite deconditioned, this movement may be fatiguing. Nonetheless, folks often enjoy this practice because it provides them with the sense that they have done something significant. I usually do three sets to begin with.

Special Preparation: You will need room to move the arms away from the body to form a T. Therefore, this particular practice might not be practical to do with a group if you are in a tight space.

Script

Sitting with your back straight and your feet on the floor... notice your breath... give yourself a moment to inhale and exhale.

Place your hands in front of you, about chest height... with your fingertips touching... your palms facing the floor as if you are about to wipe a table with your hands... and your elbows bent.

Demonstrate the action.

Inhale the arms horizontally out to the sides until your arms are in a T position... Now... exhale your arms back in... let's repeat this two more times, coordinating your breath with your movement.

Demonstrate the movement.

Inhale... arms out... exhale... arms in... inhale... exhale... notice how your arms feel moving in this plane... do you feel the weight of your arms?... inhale... exhale... is the movement tiring?

Notice how you feel.

PRACTICE 8
SQUARE BREATHING

Time: 2-4 minutes

Description: Square breathing is a commonly used variation of diaphragmatic breathing that can be done at any point during a session. It involves linking the four sides of a square with the four parts of the breath (the inhale, the exhale, and two pauses in between). Visualizing a square makes this process satisfying and manageable. In her book, *Dare to Lead*, Brené Brown (2018) includes a version of this breath called box breathing. Although the practice asks you to count to four for each part of the breath, you can reduce this to a three-count breathing pattern if four counts seems too much. In time, there may be interest in learning more about the breath. When your client has tried simple nasal breathing, is aware of their breath pattern, and is ready to try a more involved pattern, square breathing is a good next step. Eventually, you may begin to extend your breath count all the way to six and still feel comfortable. A breathing pattern is a process to explore, not a goal to attain.

Script

I am going to "conduct" this breath to give you a visual,
and once you get the hang of the pattern, you can
ignore me and envision your own square.

There are four sides to the square and four parts to
the breath: the inhale, the pause after the inhale, the
exhale, and the pause after the exhale.

Demonstrate moving your hands as if you are tracing a square in the air.

Inhale, two, three, four… pause, two, three, four… exhale,
two, three, four… pause, two, three, four.

And again, inhale, two, three, four… pause, two, three,
four… exhale, two, three, four… pause, two, three, four.

Once more, inhale, two, three, four… pause, two, three,
four… exhale, two, three, four… pause, two, three, four.

And release, returning to regular in-and-out breathing.

Notice how you are feeling.

PRACTICE 9
TUNE IN WITH THE CHIME

Time: 2 minutes

Description: A chime is a simple and affordable tool that I take to every session. I use it at the beginning of a practice to signal that we are shifting our attention and turning our outward gaze inward. I do not use it to get people to stop talking or to get their attention, although I have seen it used this way. I prefer to use listening to the chime as a practice. Over time, clients associate the sound of the chime in this manner and settle into the practice rather than simply refraining from talking. The sound of the chime signals the mind and body to tune in to itself. I connect hearing the sound of the chime with noticing (not changing—just noticing) one's breathing. The tone itself is pleasant to most ears.

I often pair this practice with centering (chapter 7, practice 3) and grounding (chapter 7, practice 4), but it can be used as a stand-alone practice. The ritual of ringing the chime is also a good way to begin a session. My regular clients know this ritual, but I always explain the process for new clients. I will sometimes sound the chime more than once—up to three times for a settling in effect. When I'm working with children and adults with intellectual disabilities, I will sometimes make using the chime a game to find out the amount of time each person can hear the chime (they raise their hand when they *can't* hear the chime anymore), which has worked well (see Variation below).

I initially felt a little awkward using the chime in individual sessions until I was given enough feedback to realize that it really was very helpful. Clients needed and wanted a signal both to begin the session and to let go of what they were previously doing. If you are doing this practice with a group, be ready and know what it is you want to do next so you can make the most of the experience of silence you have given the group. There is a chance they haven't experienced group silence together before. It is a beautiful thing. Don't be quick to use more words. Absorb the silence for a few more breaths before giving your next instruction.

Script

This is my chime. I would like to begin our time
together today with listening to the chime.

*Hold up the chime. If this session is a client's first time,
then explain the process and why you are doing it.*

Ringing this chime is how we will begin our session.
As we listen together, let's also notice our breathing.

No need to make any changes. Simply notice
that you are breathing in this moment.

Hold up the chime.

Let's listen together.

Sound the chime. Stay silent for at least thirty seconds, or longer (about a minute or so) if everyone is tracking with you.

Breathing in and breathing out… I breathe in… I breathe out… simply notice your breath.

Variation:

In just a moment, I will sound the chime again. Your job is to listen as hard as you can, and when you no longer hear the chime, raise your hand.

Since we are all different, I expect that our hearing is different too. So focus on what you hear. Ready to listen?

Sound the chime and wait. All will become quiet. It is amazing. Notice the silence together, and be ready to roll with the next instruction—before it gets noisy again.

Do you hear the silence?… it is beautiful… thank you for listening with me.

Notice how the silence feels in your body.

PRACTICE 10
STAIRSTEP BREATHING

Time: 5 minutes

Description: Stairstep breathing may seem complex at first, and that is partly the point of teaching it. The mind needs something to latch onto. I first learned this practice from Amy Weintraub, an experienced yoga therapist, trainer, author, and founder of the LifeForce Yoga Healing Institute. She describes the context of the practice this way: It is like giving a dog a bone. Before giving your dog a bone, the dog may be very distracted, but after getting the bone, the dog is focused on the bone. Because there is more to this breath than simply breathing in and out through the nose, it gives the mind something to do. Busy minds enjoy this exercise.

Use the script, and don't make it more complex than it is. Most people pick it up right away, and I reassure those who don't get it that it will get easier, as does any practice. If a client at least understands the mechanics of the breath, then they can try it again later without your guidance, which is the goal of learning the practice in the first place. Focusing the mind on the breath and slowing the repetitions switches the autonomic nervous system to its parasympathetic function.

I recommend introducing stairstep breathing during the second half or toward the end of a session. It is not the first breathing practice I introduce given its complexity. Instead, start with something easier, such as nasal breathing, and gradually build up to stairstep breathing. Be confident in your ability to lead this practice, and others will follow your lead. I use my hand to "conduct" this breath, making an action as if my hand is climbing up a set of stairs, pausing at the top, and then smoothly coming down an elevator. Even though I tell clients they don't have to conduct the breath, often they want to do the hand action with me. I no longer tell them they don't have to. The action seems to help them do the exercise. As with any of the practices, I am simply making an invitation; opting out is fine. If they opt out, then I say, "Watch me so you can get the mechanics of the breath and eventually try this on your own." It is good to continue planting the seed that they will indeed try this practice on their own.

Some people catch on to the complexity of this breath in a surprisingly short time. It is often a standout of our time together. I think people are hungry for a bit of a challenge, but one with which they have a reasonable chance of being successful. Some of my older veterans have even reported teaching stairstep breathing to their spouse or family members because it worked so well to help them calm themselves.

Caution: Do not practice this if you have had recent chest or abdominal surgery (Weintraub, 2012).

Script

Sitting up straight, spine tall, chest lifted... feet on the floor.

Let's try stairstep breathing... I will demonstrate the breath first so you can see and hear what it looks and sounds like... we take four little sips of air through the nose to make one complete inhalation, going up the stairs... pause for a moment... and exhale down the elevator.

Demonstrate the breath by taking four sips of air in and, at the same time, move your hand as if it is moving up stairs one at a time. Your hand is lifting up a few inches and then moving a few inches to the right for each step and each sip of the inhale. Then lower your hand smoothly like an elevator for the exhale.

Now let's try it together. We are going to breathe in and out of the nose, taking four little sips of air through the nose to make one complete breath... and inhale a little on each step... pause and... exhale.

As you breathe, repeat the motion of moving your hand up the stairs one at a time for each of the little inhales (sips); then smoothly lowering your hand on the exhale.

Now that we know what it feels like, let's try it all together three times on the count of three... One, two, three... inhale...

Continue to demonstrate your hand moving up the stairs.

You now have a full lung of air... pause for a moment... and then exhale slowly and smoothly... through the nose.

Demonstrate by pausing with your hand and then letting it lower down smoothly, like an elevator.

Four little sips of air... pause... exhale down...

Demonstrate hand action of climbing steps.

Exhale.

Demonstrate with hand moving downward.

And again... inhale... pause... exhale.

Demonstrate with hand.

Return to a natural breath... noticing how you feel.

PRACTICE 11
SOUNDING THE GONG

Time: 3 minutes

Description: The *ng* sound (as in the *ng* in *singing*) is a *bija* (meaning *seed*) sound and is one of the universal tones in Sanskrit, an ancient Indian language that is sometimes called the language of yoga. The *ng* sound is calming to many. Saying *ng* can be facilitated by putting your tongue on the roof of your mouth and breathing out through the nose, making the *ng* sound. While making the *ng* sound, I also sweep my arms out from my sides toward the sky, bringing my palms together above my head and then lowering my hands to my heart. If you feel a little self-conscious trying this practice at first, don't worry; you are in good company. I felt the same way. But after trying it, I noticed it was a calming practice for me, so I decided to continue doing it. Sometimes you simply have to try a practice more than once to see if it's right for you and to notice its effect. Although it's calming for me, it may be energizing for others depending on the time of day, the sensitivity of their nervous system, or other variables. But once you have ascertained how the practice affects you, you will have enough information to intelligently teach it to others.

This practice can be used anytime, but I often use it toward the end of a session as we are finding an appropriate point to conclude. Because this practice involves sound, and thereby may evoke self-consciousness, I introduce other practices first and build up to this one. I find that people are more willing to follow your lead on a practice that sounds or looks a little strange after they have found some positive effect or relief from other practices. Of course, that advice could apply to many of the practices in this book, but these feelings of awkwardness and uncertainty are a typical part of the learning process. There have been times when making this *ng* sound in a group seemed just plain funny, and the practice elicited giggling and snorting. I find that a little levity goes a long way and can help folks relax and feel more comfortable with, and receptive to, the learning process. After all, it is well established that laughter decreases stress hormones, such as cortisol. So why not indulge it when you can? Eventually, you will be able to perform this practice with a straight face. I find it to be a powerful practice and worthy of inclusion in your toolbelt.

Special Preparation: Make sure there is enough room for clients to sweep their arms up. If you are doing this exercise in a group and someone is not comfortable participating, reassure them that listening to the sound is beneficial as well.

Script

We are going to try some hand movements accompanied by a sound.
Vocalizing, which is sometimes called toning, creates a vibration
in the body. Let's just practice making a sound with
something very simple, like vowels A-E-I-O-U.

Open your mouth and place your fingers on your throat so you can feel your
vocal cords as you say, "Aaa-Eee-Iii-Ooo-Uuu." Good.
That was easy… Can you feel the vibrations?

Place your hand on your throat.

Now the sound we are going to make right now is ng… here's
how you do it: Put your tongue on the roof of your
mouth and breathe out through your nose while
making the sound… ng…good.

Let's try that again so you get the hang of it… ng…
like a soothing gong… very good.

Now let's add an arm movement… inhale and sweep the
arms up from your sides toward the sky… bring your
palms together overheard… sound ng on the exhale…
lower your hands to your heart center like this.

Demonstrate the action and the sound.

Let's do one more practice run… inhale… sweep your
arms up overheard and ng to heart center.

Sweep your arms up over head and bring them to heart center.

Let's do it three times together… inhale… sweep the arms up and ng to
heart center… inhale… sweep the arms up and ng to heart center… and
one more… inhale… sweep the arms up and ng to heart center.

Notice how you feel.

PRACTICE 12
PUSH THE PAUSE BUTTON

Time: 2 minutes

Description: Pausing a conversation can be done anytime. I have found that sometimes a client has a lot to say, and that can be a good thing. But there are times in a session when my client is using more words than I can take in. Intentionally slowing down the flow of words helps you and your client absorb what has been said. Perhaps the words need to be reflected. Perhaps clarification is needed, or perhaps you (and they) simply need to take a breath.

You may need to give a little instruction if you are just starting out. Tell your client that you may be occasionally "pushing the pause button" so you can better reflect on what you just heard. Otherwise, some people feel the need to fill every space (or pause) with more words. If you are doing this technique in a group, then your instruction is even more important so each person knows that pausing is not an opportunity to fill the space with words. Instead, it is an opportunity for silent listening.

When we allow for, and become accustomed to, pausing a conversation (or a therapy session), we slow down. Pausing literally gives us the space to think for a moment (or two) before responding, instead of reacting without thinking. These moments of thoughtful quietude can improve how we interact with the people around us and with the world in general.

This practice is done in conjunction with other practices. Use the practice of pausing to slow down the pace of whatever is happening in front of you. Use it like your own personal pause button. I even have made some buttons with the universal symbol for pause on them—for example, || (like the *equals* sign but standing vertically instead of horizontally). As you practice pausing, you will become familiar with how it feels. You may want to begin inserting a little pause between your inhale and your exhale. Then add another little pause between your exhale and your inhale. Pausing is nearly always accompanied by noticing. *How am I doing in this moment? How did it feel to inhale and exhale through my nose?*

Watch out for your own tendency to unnecessarily fill up spaces with words, instead of allowing for a silent pause. Is there a feeling arising that you would rather just dissipate or avoid altogether, such as sadness or grief? If so, then pause as a way of resolving this issue. Pausing takes practice. Our inability to pause may require some self-inquiry.

Script

Let's practice pausing together and see how it feels. I have a hand signal that I use; I raise my hand to shoulder height – like the universal sign for stop – except that my hand is still close to my body (my elbow is bent, not outstretched). This is my nonverbal way of inviting you to pause for a moment. You can feel free to use the gesture if you would like to pause when I am speaking. I will make the gesture and then say, "I'd like us to pause for a moment and absorb what you just said."

> *Make the stop gesture, elbow bent. Then track the silence for at least thirty seconds before saying anything else. Then have them make the gesture if they would like to.*

We just created some space together. How did that feel to you?

PRACTICE 13
COHERENT BREATHING

Time: 5-10 minutes

Description: Coherent breathing brings balance to the nervous system. It is a deep, rhythmic breathing practice developed by Stephen Elliott (2005) that involves taking five breaths per minute, with each breath consisting of an inhale for six seconds and an exhale for six seconds. This equates to about a four or five-count inhale and exhale (since a count of one is not equal to one second). Research has found that this practice slows the breath and resting heart rate significantly (Streeter et al., 2018).

The practice can be best explained by an example: If we typically breathe twelve to fifteen breaths per minute, then the practice of slowing down the breath to five breaths per minute will take some practice. Over time, it can universally bolster one's nervous system through its activation of the parasympathetic branch. Our thoughts slow down. We become calm. Try this exercise every day or multiple times a day during periods of stress. It is a predictable and rhythmic breathing practice that brings our attention to the present moment by focusing on the body.

Script

Sitting in your chair… spine straight… feet on the floor, hip-width apart. Notice your breath… with your mouth closed… breathe in gently and smoothly through the nose for six seconds… four… three… two… one… do not overfill the lungs.

Breathe out just as gently and smoothly… for six seconds… four… three… two… one… there's no need to expel air forcefully… the sensation is like watching the shoreline waves gently coming in and out with the tide… slow and even… predictable.

Again, inhale… four… three… two… one… and exhale… four… three… two… one… Beautiful.

Continue this pattern for five minutes.

Keep track of time for whatever amount of time you and your client (or the group) agree to. It will feel like a very long time. It is ok to start smaller and build up to five minutes. About halfway through, you can say the following:

Continue to breathe… and at the same time, if you can, notice how you feel… observe the physical sensations in your body… what do you notice?

Whatever it is… something or nothing at all… just notice what you notice.

PRACTICE 14
RATIO BREATHING

Time: 3 minutes

Description: Ratio breathing refers to inhaling for a specified number of seconds, then pausing (or suspending the breath) for a specified number of seconds, and then exhaling for a specified number of seconds. A simple ratio to start with is 3:2:4. The rule of thumb is to make the exhale (the last number) longer than your inhale (the first number). A longer exhale, even one that is slightly longer, stimulates the parasympathetic branch of the nervous system and calms the nervous system.

The pause in between is just that: a pause. I prefer to call it a pause, though many practitioners call it a hold or suspension. My reason for this is that I want no effort exerted for the pause. The word *suspend* or *hold* connotes effort to me. The idea is that you are not trying to extend the pause in any way. It is a natural break between your inhale and your exhale. If you notice yourself making little chipmunk cheeks during the pause, you are trying too hard. Back off a little. Make the pause shorter.

After your client is familiar with, and finds benefit from, this simple pattern, try a more challenging one. For example, the 4:7:8 ratio is one that Andrew Weil, a Harvard-trained physician and holistic practitioner, has popularized. However, I do not consider this a beginning breathing ratio. I think it takes quite a bit of practice to succeed with this breath. Therefore, start smaller and consider a longer breathing ratio as something to aim for down the road. I have included two different ratio breathing practices with different instructions (mostly a difference in the exhalation from the mouth).

Script

3:2:4 Variation:

Sitting comfortably in your chair… back straight… chest lifted… feet on the floor, hip-width apart… notice your breathing… if you are not already breathing in and out through your nose, do so.

Notice the pace of your breath… is it slow?… or is it fast?… or somewhere in between?

We are going to try a 3:2:4 ratio breathing pattern. This means we will inhale for three seconds, pause for two seconds, and exhale through the nose for four seconds… nice and simple.

Let's try it three times on the count of three. One, two, three... inhale, two, three... pause... and exhale, two, three, four... and again, inhale, two, three... pause... and exhale, two, three, four... one more time... inhale, two, three... pause... and exhale, two, three, four.

Release and breathe a regular in-and-out breath.

Notice how you feel.

4:7:8 Variation:

If you would like, we can try a 4:7:8 ratio breath... this breath means we will inhale through the nose for four seconds, pause for seven seconds, and then exhale through the mouth for eight seconds.

Let's try it three times on the count of three. One, two, three... inhale through the nose... two, three, four... pause, two, three, four, five, six, seven... and exhale through the mouth... two... three... four... five... six... seven and eight.

And again, inhale through the nose... two, three, four... pause, two, three, four, five, six, seven... and exhale through the mouth... two... three... four... five... six... seven and eight.

Last one, inhale through the nose... two, three, four... pause, two, three, four, five, six, seven... and exhale through the mouth... two... three... four... five... six... seven and eight.

For Both Variations:

Return to your typical breathing... notice how you are feeling.

At first, you may feel out of breath at the pause. This is common. It will get easier with practice. When I find a ratio of breathing that I like or that feels comfortable, I practice that one. I find that a good time to practice is when I am waiting somewhere. I practice in the grocery store line, at the bank, at traffic lights (but not if I am super tired), while riding the bus, or waiting for an appointment. Think about where and when you can practice next.

(Oh sorry, I didn't mean to wake you).

PRACTICE 15
ENERGY GLOBES

Time: 3-4 minutes

Description: The practice of energy globes is based on a *Qi Gong* exercise. I first learned this practice from Leah Kalish, who was the director of Yoga Ed when I was at the beginning of my journey of teaching yoga to children. I invite you to bring your playful self to this practice as well, regardless of whether you are working with children. The movement is simple, and the imaginative part is plain and accessible. The movement begins by rubbing your hands together until you can feel some heat (real, not imagined). Then you imagine that you are shaping the energy you just created into a globe, and that sphere grows big enough to break into two globes, and you hold one in each hand. Then you move your hands containing the two globes one at a time, up and then down, synchronized with the breath.

The simplicity of the movement, along with the visual of synchronizing the movement with the breath, is often powerfully calming and stabilizing. The more you offer these practices to your clients, the more they will expect you to offer opportunities for intentional breathing and movement. This practice can be done in session whenever you would like to see if your client can slow down their thoughts and breath.

Script

Let's try something called energy globes. It's fun and surprisingly interesting.
We are going to begin by rubbing our hands together.
First, go slowly... then see if you can pick up a little speed.

> *Start rubbing your palms together, slowly at first,
> and then faster until you feel some heat.*

Do you feel some heat yet?... keep rubbing... good... now separate your hands
just a little so they are about half an inch apart, with your
palms facing each other, and see what you notice.

> *Pull your hands about half an inch apart.*

Do you feel that?... what is that... that you have just created?

It's energy, and that energy is called heat... now
imagine your globe of energy expanding.

> *Move your hands out wider to make space for a bigger imaginary
> ball. Your hands will be about twelve inches apart.*

As your imaginary globe expands more, pretend to divide
it into two imaginary globes, one for each hand.

Now use one hand to lift one new globe up to about shoulder height, and
then turn your wrist, gently grasping the globe (so as not to
drop it) toward the floor... At the same time, the other hand is
grasping the other globe and is moving up to shoulder
height and then moving down, both synchronized.

**Demonstrate moving the imaginary globes
up and down in an oscillating pattern.**

Once you have the movement of the globes going smoothly, see
if you can synchronize your breath with your arm movement.

Inhale as you lift one imaginary globe up, and exhale as you move it down...
nice and slow... don't drop them... do this for
several more breaths in silence.

The next time your imaginary globes pass by each
other, let them combine back into one globe.

Demonstrate the globes consolidating.

The globe is getting smaller... until your hands are
together and you can rub them again.

Now take that energy you have created and put it somewhere. Perhaps a part
of you that needs a little more tender loving care (TLC) today.

Move your hands to a part of your body that needs TLC.

Decide where you need TLC, and put your hands there.
Perhaps it is your heart, your mind, or your knee.

Take a few more inhales and exhales... release your hands.

And shake them out... notice how you feel... what did you notice?

PRACTICE 16
NECK SURRENDER

Time: 3-5 minutes

Description: The neck and shoulders are very common places where we hold tension in the body. Therefore, paying some regular attention to these areas can go a long way toward combating chronic tension. This practice involves very slow neck movements, coordinated with the breath. That's it! Even though we know this type of practice is good for us, it can still be hard to remember to do it. My suggestion is that you set an hourly timer to remind yourself to get up from your chair, or whatever activity you are engaged in, and move your body. Take a few deep breaths. Then do this practice at least once a day. Try doing this practice slower than slow (whatever that is for you). It really does take practice to move this slowly. Underwhelm yourself a little. I recommend that you introduce this practice into session as needed. When you feel comfortable adding movement, you may want to add this one early on to help relieve neck tension that is common with so many of us.

Script

Begin by sitting comfortably in your chair… back straight… feet on the
floor… chest lifted in Chair Mountain… notice your neck and shoulders.

We are going to give your neck a little treat for a few minutes.
Think about the work it does supporting your head and your
brain. The average head weighs seven to eight pounds.
That is a lot of weight to hold up every day.

Decide whether it is better for your back today to use the back of the
chair for support, or to sit on the edge of your chair letting your
back support itself with help from your legs and abdominal
muscles…either is fine… if you choose the first option,
make sure that your bottom is all the way against the
back of the chair so you are not tempted to slouch.

Choose one posture or the other.

Before we do this movement, let me demonstrate so you don't need
to look up when your gaze should be toward the floor instead. I am
dropping my chin toward my chest… the movement is the same as if I
were drawing a smiley face across my chest with my chin… Begin with
an inhale… Move your chin toward one shoulder, always moving within
your pain-free range of motion… pause if you feel some resistance…
exhale… chin back to center… then inhale… chin toward
the other shoulder… exhale back to center.

Demonstrate this movement with your neck.

We will repeat this movement. A note of instruction… you don't have to feel any sensation when you move your neck… in fact, it is best if you don't. Simply breathe and move… even if you experience no sensation at all.

Find your breath… lower your chin to your chest… and inhale… shift your chin toward one shoulder, moving within your pain-free range of motion… exhale back to center.

And again… inhale… chin travels toward the other shoulder… and exhale… return to center.

One more time… inhale… chin travels toward the shoulder… and exhale… return to center.

Good… gently bring the chin up… put your hand under your chin, with your palm facing down… Check that your palm is parallel to the floor… good.

Demonstrate putting your hand under your chin, palm down. Then relax your hand, placing it back at your side.

Now inhale and rotate your head to the right… exhale and return center… inhale and rotate your head to the left… exhale and return center… and again, nice and slowly… inhale right… exhale center… inhale left… exhale center.

These are your last directions for movement. Again, underwhelm yourself… this is your neck. Remember all the weight it bears to support your head… be kind to it… inhale and tilt your right ear toward your right shoulder… don't force it… just head (pun intended) in that direction… exhale and return to center.

Inhale and tilt your left ear toward your left shoulder… very gently… exhale and return to center.

Notice how your neck is feeling… do you notice any difference?

PRACTICE 17
SIGHING BREATH

Time: 2 minutes

Description: The action of sighing—and its accompanying movement: shrugging—is a natural manner in which the body responds to difficult information. Sighing is familiar to most of us and usually happens involuntarily. By comparison, the sighing breath is done intentionally. Adding some arm movement places some emphasis on something we are already feeling. Even if you or your client do little movement, it probably will feel good to sigh in this way, and it is super easy to do. For this reason, sighing breath may be a good starting point because it is common to all of us and can be beneficial to introduce early in a session. It can also be a good transition practice. Sighing serves as a signal that the body is dissipating energy, or moving on.

Script

Let's begin by noticing how you are feeling right now... what is your breath doing?... are you breathing long breaths or short breaths?

Sighing breath is just like it sounds. Let's practice the sighing part... just like this... sigh.

> *Demonstrate sighing.*

Try it again... sigh... good... now let's add an arm movement.
It goes like this: Inhale the arms up to the sky, and then sigh them back down to your lap.

> ***Demonstrate inhaling the arms up in front of you and exhaling (sighing) them down.***

Now that you have the hang of it, let's try it three times... on the count of three. One, two, three, inhale the arms up... exhale, sigh them down... and again, inhale the arms up and exhale, sigh them down... one more time, inhale the arms up... exhale, sigh them down... and again, inhale the arms... up and exhale, sigh them down.

Good, relax your hands... notice your breath.

CHAPTER 7

BALANCING PRACTICES

I use the term *balancing* here in several ways. Some of the practices, such as Tree Pose, are about balancing on one foot, which is a practice that highlights the physical balancing of one's body weight. Some practices are about balancing energy and are helpful when you notice that your states of energy are fluctuating haphazardly—physically, emotionally, or both. Irregular states of energy may be a signal that you need to take a break and rest, or it could mean that you need a balancing practice, such as alternate nostril breathing, to even out your energy. Remember, though, that alternate nostril breathing may serve as a calming practice instead of a balancing one. Indeed, many of the practices in this section, such as the different Movements of the Spine (Seated Cat-Cow, lateral movement, and spinal twists), could just as logically be placed in the chapters on calming practices or energizing practices. As you and your clients become familiar with each individual practice and with your experience with the practice, it will become clearer to you in which pocket of your toolbelt the practice belongs. The fun is in exploring and developing your awareness as you go along.

Keep in mind that your clients may not experience each practice the same way that you do. A balancing practice that is calming for you may be energizing for them and vice versa. Therefore, whenever you introduce a new practice, it is important to get feedback from the client on their experience of it. This will help inform your use of that practice for them going forward.

PRACTICE 1

MOVEMENTS OF THE SPINE: SEATED CAT-COW

Time: 3-4 minutes

Description: Your spine is made to move. It needs to move through its full, pain-free range of motion *every day*, whether or not you think you need it. Along with nasal breathing, this practice is a staple in my own daily practice. It can be done anytime. Often, mornings or evenings are good times to bookend the day with moving the spine. Frequently, I will introduce this practice near the beginning of a session. It is surprising to see how a little movement goes a long way toward settling oneself for the work of talk therapy ahead. The following script is geared toward practicing this while sitting in a chair. However, you can also do this sitting crossed-legged on the floor.

Special Preparation: In a one-on-one session, you can sit across from your client or beside them, whichever feels more comfortable to your client. If you are teaching a small group where clients are sitting in a circle or horseshoe shape, place yourself where everyone can see you and you can see everyone.

Script

Your spine is made to move. It needs to move through its full, pain-free range of motion every day, whether or not you think you need it. Right now, let's move the spine in two directions: forward and backward.

Sitting comfortably in your chair, the spine is straight, the chest lifted slightly. Begin by placing your feet hip-width apart on the floor. Or you can make a one or two fist-size space between your knees.

Notice the feeling of breathing in your body… are you breathing through your nose or your mouth?… is it a short breath?… or a long breath?… if you are not already breathing in and out through the nose, do so if you can.

If you are congested today or cannot breathe in and out through your nose, just do the best you can.

Breathing in and out through the nose. Let's begin our exploration of the spine… inhale… lift the chest… arching the back a little… exhale… rounding the back a little… making a C with your spine.

> *Demonstrate the movement as you lead it.*
> *Hold your hand up making the letter C.*

We are only moving in our pain-free range of motion… link your breath to your movement… like this… inhale, lift… exhale, round… invite yourself to do a little less so you can find your breath.

> **Demonstrate lifting the chest and arching the back a little as you inhale, then rounding the back a little as you exhale.**

And again… inhale… lift the chest… arching the back a little, exhale… rounding the spine a little… good… let's keep going and repeat.

> **Continue demonstrating the movement.**

It is a smooth, flowing action… joining our flowing breath to our flowing movement… you can rest at any time… if you want to keep going, let's continue for three more… inhale, lift… exhale, round… inhale, lift… exhale, round… good… last one… inhale, lift… exhale, round.

We are all finding our own way. Your movement is your movement.

This movement is also called Seated Cat-Cow… notice how your spine is feeling… your movement may be a little more or less than mine, depending on how your back is feeling today… I'm a little stiff today, so my movement is small.

> **Or, instead, say whatever is true about your movement today.**

PRACTICE 2

MOVEMENTS OF THE SPINE: LATERAL MOVEMENT

Time: 3-4 minutes

Description: Two more movements of the spine, and a favorite of mine, are moving the spine laterally or simply from side to side. It can easily be done standing or sitting in a chair. In a group setting, you may need to coordinate the movement if you are using the extended arm version. That is, have everyone move the same way at the same time.

Special Preparation: In a one-on-one session, you can sit across from your client or beside them, whichever feels more comfortable to your client. If you are teaching a small group where clients are sitting in a circle or horseshoe shape, place yourself where everyone can see you and you can see everyone.

Script

Sitting comfortably in your chair, the spine is straight, the chest lifted slightly. Begin by placing your feet hip-width apart on the floor. Or you can make a one or two fist-size space between your knees.

Notice the feeling of breathing in your body… are you breathing through your nose or your mouth?… is it a short breath?… or a long breath?… if you are not already breathing in and out through the nose, do so if you can.

If you are congested today or cannot breathe in and out through your nose, just do the best you can.

Let's begin with two movements of the spine… laterally flexing the spine to the right and to the left… it doesn't matter which way you start.

Demonstrate moving the spine from side to side in a leaning movement.

Gently sway from side to side, shifting your body weight from one sitting bone to the other… that's it… now we can add a lever.

Place your hand on your hip.

This creates a short lever.

Place your hand on your shoulder.

This creates a medium lever.

> *Raise your left arm toward the ceiling, and gently
> lean to the right. Switch from one side to the other.*

And this creates a long lever.

As your body weight shifts from side to side, so does
the arm you are using.

As you model the actions, continue to experiment with various
levers to encourage your client to experiment as well. Eventually,
pick one and stay with it. Remember, it is generally better to do
less and to demonstrate less movement, particularly at
first, so pick the hip or shoulder lever.

You can experiment a little to see which lever feels most
comfortable for you today… then stick with that one…
whatever it is… it may be different from mine.

Remember to link your breath with your movement… let's try it three
more times on each side… pause anytime you need to… note
whether this feels good or not. If you happen to be doing
the tall lever, feel free to air high-five your neighbor.

> *Smile. Look for smiles and nods. If you don't see them,
> then pause and tell them to do less. Catch someone's eye
> (if you are in a group) and give them an air high-five.*

This movement could also easily be done standing or sitting
crossed-legged on the floor. Perhaps next time you could
try one of these other options to move the spine laterally.

Be sure to do a little of this one every day.

PRACTICE 3
MOVEMENTS OF THE SPINE: SPINAL TWISTS

Time: 3-4 minutes

Description: We can often overlook the need to rotate the spine since we don't do much twisting in our typical getting up, getting dressed, and out-the-door activities. However, this is worth intentionally adding to your daily movement so your spine gets used to what safe, gentle rotation feels like while twisting, as opposed to jerking or pushing movements. You can do this practice anytime, other than after you have just eaten, given that it may be uncomfortable to twist the spine while you are digesting food. The instructions for this practice are for sitting in a chair. But the practice could easily be done standing or sitting on the floor, much like the other movements of the spine.

Special Preparation: In a one-on-one session, you can sit across from your client or beside them, whichever feels more comfortable to your client. If you are teaching a small group where clients are sitting in a circle or horseshoe shape, place yourself where everyone can see you and you can see everyone.

Script

Sitting comfortably in your chair, the spine is straight, the chest lifted slightly. Begin by placing your feet hip-width apart on the floor. Or you can make a one or two fist-size space between your knees.

Notice the feeling of breathing in your body… are you breathing through your nose or your mouth?… is it a short breath?… or a long breath?… if you are not already breathing in and out through the nose, do so if you can.

If you are congested today or cannot breathe in and out through your nose, just do the best you can.

Let's begin two movements of the spine… twisting the spine to the right and to the left… it doesn't matter which way you start. We will practice a very slow twist, and it doesn't need to be much… try it like this… inhale and lift the chest… exhale and rotate your spine… not just your head and shoulders.

> *Demonstrate a gentle twisting action.*

When you get to the end of your exhale… pause and hold the twist… explore here for a few breaths… find a satisfying, natural in-and-out breath… good… now let's unwind the spine… coming back to center.

Twist on the exhale. It doesn't need to be much. Demonstrate restraint in the action.

Now for the other side… inhale and lift the chest… and exhale turn… find a natural stopping point in your twist and pause… now breathe a pleasant, natural in-and-out breath.

Remember, you are holding the pose… not your breath… and unwind… coming back to center.

You have now done a seated spinal twist. Let's check in here and notice how you are feeling.

Repeat the twist on both sides if you have more time.

Merryn's Story: Yoga in Unlikely Places

Sometimes teaching yoga can happen in the most unlikely places. About a year ago, my then 24-year-old daughter, Merryn, who is also a yoga teacher, traveled with me to Israel and Palestine. A Palestinian friend warned us that his Muslim family may not have heard of yoga, and he was pretty sure they would not be interested in doing yoga. However, they would certainly be interested in meeting us and showing us Arab hospitality, which included picking us up at a checkpoint, feeding us, visiting with us, giving us a place to stay, and introducing us to many family members and neighbors.

Our Palestinian friend brought a translator with him to pick us up. We spent several hours driving around the beautiful hills of Palestine, drinking lots of very strong Arabic coffee and chatting about their lives. At some point, our translator had to go to work at a local language school where he taught English. Later in the day, we returned to the school, and he introduced us to five young male Palestinians and handed a marker to my daughter, saying "The experts are here. Please teach." Never one to be slow on the uptake, Merryn jumped right in and started teaching English. I was amazed. She had the youth out of their seats and engaged in no time. Fortunately, she had been working with refugee women each week near her university, so she did have some real-life experience teaching English as a second language. Meanwhile, we all sat watching—thoroughly entertained and enjoying the lively classroom interaction. And what does this story have to do with the practices in this book, you may be thinking? Well, there's more to the story…

What happened next was truly beautiful. Merryn reached a natural stopping point in her English language instruction and simply said, "And now we are going to do some yoga." And with that, the youth all moved to the small space at the front of the classroom as Merryn seamlessly led the group in nasal breathing and Tree Pose. While having a proud mama moment, I completely forgot my professionalism and found myself standing on a desk taking pictures and videoing the encounter. I figured I might need proof. But what this story reminded me of was that if you give people an opportunity and clear instruction, they will follow your lead and experience something they have never tried before. Merryn made the experience fun and accessible. My friend and his dad were even joining in from their chairs. It was a lighthearted occasion, and the kids told us how differently they felt after practicing these very simple yoga poses and breathing exercises.

PRACTICE 4
HEART SOOTHING

Time: 2 minutes

Description: Sometimes difficult emotions can arise during a session. Pausing to acknowledge emotions as they occur or inquiring when this happens may be part of what you already do in a session. The heart soothing practice can be an additional tool for such situations. The action and movement involved in the practice are embodied ways to acknowledge feelings that arise, whatever they may be. The action is also an invitation to the body that all feelings are welcome. Finally, as the name of the practice suggests, this exercise can be soothing and is a way for clients to calm themselves in the moment. This practice can be done anytime during a session, or it can be offered when difficult emotions arise. Watch for visible signs of relaxation, such as the shoulders dropping a little or the breath slowing.

Script

Check in with your body... notice how you feel.

Let's begin by sitting up straight in the chair... place your arms out like a goalpost... elbows at right angles, if that is available to you.

Breathe here for a few beats... on the inhale, we are going to twist to the right ... bringing the left hand to the heart... and then exhale back to center, returning the arms to goalpost.

Demonstrate starting with goalpost arms, then twisting right and bringing the left hand to the heart, then returning to goalpost arms.

Let's try it in the other direction... on the inhale, twist left and bring the right hand to the heart... then exhale back to center.

Sitting with your back straight. Chest lifted. Breathing in and out through your nose... and repeat... keep it going to the rhythm of your breath... twisting to each side... inhaling and exhaling as you move.

How does it feel to move in this gentle, caring way?... is there a sense of soothing?

Notice how you feel.

PRACTICE 5
BALANCING

Time: 2-3 minutes

Description: Balancing can be as simple as standing on one foot. Perhaps even doing Tree Pose. If you are unable to balance for a few seconds on one foot, this provides useful information about yourself. It could mean that your mind is overly busy, upset, or agitated in the moment you are trying to balance. An agitated mind affects our ability to physically balance, which reinforces the principle that the mind influences the body and the body influences the mind. The good news is that you can strengthen your physical ability to balance with practice. You can do this exercise anytime during a session, either as a check-in or as a transition. If a client truly struggles with balance but wants to persevere with the exercise, remind them to pause and rest at any point. If their eyes are closed, instruct them to open their eyes. It is harder to balance with the eyes closed.

Special Preparation: Many clients find it useful to stand behind a chair and use the chair to help with balance.

Script

Let's check in for a moment... let's stand... notice
your body... feel the support of the floor.

> *Shift your weight from one foot to another.*

Now lift one foot an inch or two off the floor... even just a little...
balance on the other foot... breathe... hold the chair for
support if you want. Taking a few breaths here... inhale
and exhale... breathing in and breathing out.

Lower your foot to the floor... let's see if it is any different
on the other side.... lift the other foot... balance...
breathe... hold the chair if you want.

Inhale... exhale... breathing in and breathing out... and again.

Lower your foot to the floor... good... let's try lifting your foot
again, and this time rest the sole of your foot below your
knee, along the inside edge of your shin. This is Tree Pose.

Demonstrate lifting the foot and placing it beneath the knee. Place your hands together, with your palms touching, at your heart center. If the client is struggling to balance, suggest they simply lift the heel off the ground and let the toe remain on the floor for balance. Or they can hold on to the chair or wall with one hand for support, pressing the other hand into heart center.

Your foot also can rest above the knee on the inside surface of the thigh, just not on the knee joint itself… this is because it would create too much pressure on the knee joint… Choose to hold on to the chair or bring your hands together at your heart center. Or instead of lifting your foot, simply lift your heel off the floor, letting your toe stay on the floor, more like Sapling Pose. Whichever you choose, it is all good for improving your ability to balance.

Demonstrate putting your other foot below the knee. Or try Sapling Pose.

If you would like to, you can lift your arms over your head or reach your arms into a V while continuing to breathe… stare at a fixed focal point to steady yourself.

Notice your breathing… and release the pose… let's try it on the other side.

Bring your hands to your heart center… lift your arms over your head.

Demonstrate the action of Sapling Pose on the other side. Either bring your hands to your heart center or lift your arms overhead.

Breathe… and release. Balance improves over time.

I often use this practice during the day, including when cleaning my teeth, making sandwiches, stirring soup, waiting for the bus, or standing in line. Think about where you can practice.

PRACTICE 6
ALTERNATE NOSTRIL BREATHING

Time: 3-4 minutes

Description: Alternate nostril breathing is generally a calming practice, but there are always outliers who find the practice energizing. For this reason, it is a good idea for you to practice this tool first so you know how it affects you. I have taught this breath to children as young as five and to people in their nineties. It is my go-to practice for preparing for sleep (and for getting back to sleep if I wake up in the middle of the night). I find it more interesting than counting sheep and it requires my mind to focus. The mind gets quiet when it is encouraged to focus on one thing and one thing only.

You can use this practice anytime during a session, and it is particularly useful if your client mentions problems with resting or sleeping. Explain the mechanics of the breath and how to use the hands, and make sure to only complete a few rounds since it can have an immediate, calming effect on the nervous system. Too many repetitions and you will have everyone snoozing or saying that yoga makes them tired. Let clients know that less is more and that they are learning the practice until it becomes smoother and easier to use when they need it.

Special Preparation: In addition to practicing while seated in a chair, alternate nostril breathing can be practiced while lying in bed at home.

Script

Sit up straight in the chair... notice how you are feeling.

Put the index and middle fingers of your right hand together.

> *Demonstrate by holding up the index
> and middle fingers of your right hand.*

Place the tips of these two fingers against the skin between your eyebrows... As you do this... you will notice that your ring finger and thumb are in a position to close one nostril at a time.

> *Demonstrate placing the index finger and middle finger
> between the eyebrows and waggling your thumb and ring finger.*

For this version of alternate nostril breathing... let's close the left nostril with the ring finger... inhale through the right nostril... pause... exhale through the right nostril.

Release the left nostril, and close the right nostril with the thumb... inhale through the left nostril... pause... exhale through the left nostril... release the right nostril... close the left nostril with the ring finger.

You will get the hang of this breath after a few rounds... inhale right... pause... exhale right.

Let's repeat alternate nostril breathing for a few more rounds.

Continue to demonstrate.

Check in with yourself... notice the effect on your nervous system.

Quick Variation:

Simply close the right nostril and breathe only through the left nostril for several minutes. This practice is generally very calming.

PRACTICE 7
SEATED PIGEON

Time: 2 minutes

Description: Seated Pigeon is an accessible modification of a more challenging version that is done on the floor. The point of doing the pose from a chair is to externally rotate one hip at a time, an important action that is missing from regular standing and sitting activities. Many people (myself included) are not particularly aware of their hips, but functional hip mobility is essential to many daily activities, such as getting dressed and moving around. Therefore, rotating your hips is certainly a helpful action to assist you in putting your pants on in the morning. Keeping your ball-and-socket joint mobile may be good for your emotional health too. For many years and from different teachers, I have heard the phrase "negative emotions are stored in the hips." I haven't seen a study corroborating this possibility, but I have practiced yoga long enough to know there is so much more than I can possibly study. The ancient wisdom of the yogis may be on to something.

Seated Pigeon can be introduced or practiced anytime during session. Daily practice is recommended. Many people have tight hip flexors and will not have a huge range of motion in their hips. Others will have hypermobility. Often these folks do not *feel* the pose. Reassure them that it is fine if they do not feel the pose. Simply being in the pose, even without feeling sensation in doing so, is a good practice. Whether someone is feeling sensation or not, the point is that the hip is externally rotating.

Script

Begin by sitting straight in your chair with your feet flat on the floor in
Chair Mountain… your feet are hip-width apart… toes tracking forward.

Notice your hips… feel your sitting bones on the chair… direct your
attention into the hip joints themselves… how do they feel right
now?… it's okay if you don't notice anything in particular.

Now lift your right ankle and rest it on your left knee… don't strain… if
it doesn't go there easily, then let your foot slide down onto your shin.

Demonstrate both options.

Observe the pace of your breath… if you want to explore your
hip joint a bit… put your right hand on your right knee and
gently guide your knee slightly toward the floor.

Remember, we always move in our pain-free range of motion. The
movement we are doing will bring some awareness to your hip joints.

Look for tension in the face or holding of the breath.

Return to observing your breath… don't force the movement… take five natural breaths here.

Now uncross the foot, and place it back on the floor… notice how the hip you just externally rotated feels.

Let's try it on the other side… from your Chair Mountain… lift your left foot and place it on your right knee… if that position is available to you. If not, try resting your foot on your shin.

Demonstrate both options.

Notice your breath… just as on the other side… if you want to explore your hip more deeply… you can put your left hand on your left knee and gently move your knee toward the floor, externally rotating the joint.

Focus again on the flow of your breath… don't force the movement in your hip… take five natural breaths here.

Now uncross the foot, and place it back on the floor.

Notice if there were any differences between the range of movement on the left and the right side… notice sensations of increased circulation.

PRACTICE 8
EAGLE WINGS

Time: 3-4 minutes

Description: There are two versions of this pose. Both involve crossing the arms at the midline of the body, though the second variation also creates some space between the shoulder blades. Some studies suggest that crossing the midline of the body activates the opposite hemisphere of the brain, so cross-lateral movement might promote balance via this activation (Hannaford, 1995). This action doesn't have to be particularly energetic but can consist of simply crossing the midline of the body from side to side. The action can be done with the arms or the legs. Many yoga poses already include this component, such as tapping across the midline (practice 12 in this chapter). I find this practice useful when my clients feel stuck, physically or emotionally. If you do this practice while standing and you cross your feet, it can be difficult to find balance even though both feet are on the floor.

Despite the simplicity of the movement, it can be surprisingly challenging if someone's ability to perceive where they are in space is compromised. Therefore, if your client is eager to try the practice and starts to fumble with arm or wrist crossing, be prepared to pause the action and guide them through the movements step by step. The finger, wrist, arm, and shoulder movements can also raise awareness of tender spots in these areas that might be the result from prolonged screen time or time behind the driver's wheel.

Script

First Variation:

> Begin sitting in Chair Mountain or standing tall... notice
> the pace of your breathing... bring awareness to your
> fingers... wrists... arms and shoulders.
>
> If you have never tried this pose before... let's begin moving
> step by step until your body gets the hang of it... let's lift the
> arms straight out in front of you to chest height, arms straight...
> Pretend that you are holding a doorknob in each hand, and
> turn the knobs to the left and to the right... inhaling turns the
> knobs to the left... exhaling turns them to the right.

Demonstrate the movement. Arms should be straight, with wrists and shoulders rotated slightly to simulate the action of twisting a doorknob.

We don't usually have our wrists and arms in these positions… so at first it may take a little conscious maneuvering… we may get information from our body along the way about muscle tightness or stiffness in the joints of the arms, shoulders, and wrists… Think of all the new ways we now use our hands, wrists, and fingers with how we interact with screens.

Now cross your wrists in front of your body with your arms extended… your palms are facing down… now rotate your palms inward toward one another and interlace your fingers together.

Bending your elbows, draw your interlaced hands and fingers toward your heart.

Demonstrate the movement.

Good… breathe… notice your fingers, wrists, arms, and shoulders.

Second Variation:

Begin by sitting or standing straight and tall… cross your arms in front of your chest and hold on to the opposite elbow.

Demonstrate crossing arms in front of chest and holding elbows.

Now move your fingers up your arms a little… if you are able… and give your biceps and triceps a little squeeze.

Now keeping your arms crossed, move your fingers up toward your shoulders … if you can… until it feels like you are giving yourself a hug.

Demonstrate squeezing biceps and triceps and then moving hands toward the shoulders.

Good… now notice if you have room to lift your elbows a little… how are your shoulder blades doing?… how does it feel to be held?… you can move your body a little… perhaps a little rocking motion… notice your ribs expanding as you breathe in and out.

Notice which arm is on top… uncross the arms, and put the other arm on top.

Demonstrate uncrossing the arms and putting the other arm on top.

Massage those biceps and triceps… now move the fingers up the shoulders… and hug yourself… Receive your own hug… feel your ribcage expanding in and out with your breath.

Uncross your arms.

Balancing
Practices

PRACTICE 9
SEATED INVERSION

Time: 4-7 minutes

Description: The term *inversion* might conjure up images of bendy, slim people doing headstands and handstands. It's true that headstands and handstands are part of a family of yoga poses called inversions, but that's not what I am proposing here. The definition of an inversion is simply to position your head below your heart—even slightly. In understanding this broader definition of an inversion, a world of possibilities opens up that makes inversions accessible for almost anyone.

A seated inversion is the closest approximation I can find to having a reset button for my brain. The freshly oxygenated blood that flushes my brain when my head is below my heart is both stimulating and calming. For me, the practice belongs in the middle pocket of my toolbelt. Though your experience of the practice may be different from mine, I find it almost impossible to think with my head below my heart. My thoughts quiet down, which can be refreshing when I tire of the non-stop brain chatter that goes on inside my busy mind. In short, a seated inversion refreshes me.

Most people can have their head below their heart for a minute or two without feeling faint. However, if the practice feels a little weird to you, remember that *less is more*, and start very slowly—even if it lasts less than a minute. This pressure usually diminishes or disappears completely after a few weeks of practice. Over time, you can gradually increase the amount of time you can comfortably have your head below your heart. Let your breath and comfort level be your main guides. If you are not breathing easily and smoothly, then you are doing too much and need to back off a little. If you continue to feel dizzy after a few weeks of practice, perhaps this is not a practice for you.

An inversion can be done anytime during a session. The pose teaches you how to find steadiness and ease even when the world seems upside down. When I do this practice for myself, it tends to be toward the end of my workday, when I am feeling tired and frazzled. However, I don't recommend doing it too close to bedtime in case the practice is energizing for you.

Special Preparation: This practice can be done sitting in a chair or standing with your heels a few inches away from the wall, folding forward from the hips, with your bottom receiving support from the wall. If done while standing, legs can be straight or bent, depending on your hamstring flexibility. Alternatively, the practice can be done in the reverse by lying on the floor with your legs pressed up against the wall and your bottom as close to wall as possible. This lying down version can be helpful if you have high blood pressure and is very restful.

Caution: If you have a headache or are congested, this may not be a good time to do this pose. However, some people report that doing an inversion soothes their headache and relieves congestion. If you have glaucoma or detached retinas, or if you are pregnant or have unmedicated high blood pressure, this practice is not for you.

Script

Sitting comfortably in your chair... with your feet hip-width apart... bring your hands to the sides of your hips. Notice your breath... notice how you are feeling... what is the speed of your mind chatter?... place your hands on your legs. You are going to slide your hands down your legs toward the floor... leaning forward over your legs and knees.

Demonstrate by placing your hands on your legs and sliding your hands and body toward the floor. Stop where you feel the natural resistance from your hips or back. Then push up to return to sitting straight.

We are going to do this movement three times. After the third time down, we will stay down. You will notice that your hands will either dangle comfortably on or near the floor, or if this pose feels like too much of a stretch in your spine, you will need to come back up a little and place your elbows on your knees.

Demonstrate elbows on knees, leaning forward, back rounded.

Let us begin by folding forward and sliding our hands on our legs heading toward the floor. Then to return, we will push our feet into the floor, sliding our hands along our legs and reversing back to sitting.

On the count of three. One, two, three... inhale and slowly exhale... hands on your side seams, heading toward the floor... rounding the spine forward into a seated forward fold.

Inhale... push your feet into the floor and reverse your hands along your legs... exhale... hands on your legs heading toward the floor... rounding the spine forward.

Inhale... push your feet into the floor and reverse your hands along your legs... exhale... hands on your legs heading toward the floor... rounding the spine forward.

This time consider staying down a little while... inhale... rounding the spine... where is your natural end range of folding forward that feels comfortable?... and where can you breathe smoothly?... let your hands dangle on or near the floor, or back up a little until your elbows rest comfortably on your knees... if that feels like too much forward movement in your spine, round the spine, and let your chin rest on your chest.

We are going to linger here for two minutes or so, but you can come up anytime if you wish to... when you do want to come up... do it very slowly so you do not get dizzy.

Find your breath... release the neck... try to work with gravity, not against it... release your jaw... soften your face.

Keep time. At about the one-minute mark, you can say:

If you are doing okay, no dizziness or shortness of breath, we will stay here a little longer. Most people can sustain two minutes without feeling dizzy, but you are your own best judge of whether you want to continue... remember when you come up to do so very slowly... use the strength of your legs by gently pushing your feet into the floor.

At the two-minute mark, you can say:

In just a moment, we will come back up very, very slowly... you may feel the sensation of the blood flowing back toward your heart... but don't worry if you don't... just know that that is happening... let's sit quietly... taking in and enjoying the sensations of the body as it "rights" itself... find your breath... direct your awareness into your right hand... sense into your left hand... sense into your right foot... sense into your left foot... notice your whole body... let the breath breathe you—meaning, allow the breath to happen naturally—in a way that feels supportive.

If your client is quiet and seems peaceful, offer or maintain another minute of silence.

Tune in, notice your body... if you like to meditate, note whether you think this would work as a beginning to your meditation practice... if you want to learn to meditate, then this might be a good starting point... note how you are doing in this moment... observe whether the practice was easy or hard for you... did you like or not like it?... when might you want to do this practice again?

Just sit quietly for a minute. Observe your client discreetly.

PRACTICE 10
CHIN TUCKING

Time: 2-3 minutes

Description: No doubt you have heard the term *text neck* by now. The head protrudes forward ahead of the spine, which adds extra load to the neck and back. Perhaps you yourself have experienced this painful condition. It is very common. Chin tucking is an antidote to text neck, and it is a practice that you will want to cultivate daily if you spend many hours texting, working at a computer, or driving. Or maybe you do all three. If so, then this practice will help you mitigate some of the strain and bring your ears back in line with your shoulders. The practice looks as if you are trying to make a double chin—not too hard for some of us—while elongating the back of the neck. You can benefit from doing it multiple times a day. I recommend doing this practice early in a session to release tension in the neck.

Script

This practice can be done sitting or standing. Begin by noticing your posture and your breathing… how is your neck doing right now?… what do you notice?… is there tension?… if so, where?

Let's do a little test to begin with. Simply turn your head to the right… and then to the left… notice where your shoulders are. If you can only see your shoulders in your peripheral vision and not directly in your sight line, this may indicate that your head is jutting forward.

Make a note of what you see.

Start by sitting in Chair Mountain… connect to your breath… pull your head back and up… your chin may glide toward your chest… as if making a double chin.

Demonstrate making a double chin and pulling the head back and up.

Notice as you do this action that the back of the neck lengthens… and draws your ears in line with your shoulders. A simple little turn of the head to the right or left will allow you to notice the repositioning of the head… make sure you are breathing as you do this action.

Demonstrate turning the head to the left and then to the right.

Notice if it feels peculiar to do this action. If so, it may be that your default position consists of your head protruding forward and your shoulders being rounded... which then collapses the chest and rounds the back... yes, you can still breathe in this position, but not optimally... and it certainly is not good for your neck.

> **Demonstrate head protruding forward, slight hunch of shoulders and back rounding.**

Now come back to Chair Mountain and tuck your chin... ah... that feels better. Make a double chin... lengthen the back of the neck... and breathe... try turning the head again... are you noticing any more range of motion?

Sitting at your computer or while sitting at a red light are good times to practice chin tucking.

This movement is a much better way to support your great brain. Now shrug your shoulders a few times.

Notice how your neck and shoulders feel.

PRACTICE 11
EAR SOOTHER

Time: 3-4 minutes

Description: There are many nerve endings in the ears, which makes them sensitive to sensation and touch. In fact, acupuncture is typically done on the ears because the acupressure points can be easily accessed. However, ear soother is a much more discrete practice that simply involves rubbing or massaging the ears. I once taught this practice to fourth and fifth grade boys at an alternative school, and it became a favorite because they could use it to self-soothe without drawing attention to themselves. In fact, it was so discreet that no one even knew they were doing it. Although ear soother is generally quite soothing, it can be logically placed in any of the toolbelt categories of calming, balancing, or energizing. So, pay careful attention to how you feel after you have done the practice a few times. You can introduce this practice any time the experience of self-soothing is needed. In this way, real-time feedback is possible.

Script

Sitting up straight in your chair... notice your feet on the floor... notice if there is any tension in your face... if there is, see if you can release it. Sometimes just opening and closing the mouth a few times is enough to release excess tension in the jaw.

Demonstrate opening the jaw and closing it.

Notice your ears. We are going to work with one ear at a time. Take your thumb and index finger, and rub your ear lobe—the meatiest part of your ear. If you are wearing earrings, you may need to do a workaround. Just use as much pressure as is comfortable for you.

Demonstrate rubbing one ear.

Now work your way up the ear, gently unrolling the cartilage until you get all the way to the top of the ear... explore the rolled edge... see if you can be aware of your breathing as you are doing this.

If you find that you are holding your breath, return to breathing... release your ear... rest your arm.

Notice how you feel... take a moment to notice the difference between the ear you just worked with and your unexplored ear.

Now start to work with the other ear... take your thumb and index finger, and rub your ear lobe—the meatiest part of your ear. Again, if you are wearing earrings, you may need to do a workaround. Just use as much pressure as is comfortable for you.

Demonstrate rubbing the other ear.

Now work your way up the ear, gently unrolling the cartilage until you get all the way to the top of the ear... explore the rolled edge... see if you can be aware of your breathing as you are doing this.

Notice your breathing... release your ear... rest your arm.

Notice your ear... now notice both ears.

PRACTICE 12
TAPPING ACROSS THE MIDLINE

Time: 3 minutes

Description: Tapping across the midline looks like a variation of a Jane Fonda aerobic move from the 80s—except it is done slowly and with the breath. It involves a little twisting of the torso and tapping each elbow to your opposite knee or each hand to the opposite knee. This practice can be done standing, but it is much more accessible from a sitting position. Sitting also allows the twist to be a little more organic. Even so, twisting should be done with caution. If you notice that clients are holding their breath, encourage them to breathe smoothly. Crossing the midline can be helpful in stimulating both hemispheres of the brain. This practice is useful to introduce when a client seems stuck in their thoughts or emotions.

Script

Sitting tall in your chair, with your feet on the floor... notice where you are in relationship to other things in the room... notice any sensations along your spine... notice that your spine is supported by your bottom... notice your feet on the floor.

Let's practice a little twist of the torso in each direction... only moving in the range that is available to you today and that is pain-free.

Demonstrate a little twist to the left and to the right.

Taking the next move slowly, when you twist, see if you can lift your knee just a little. If you are twisting right, lift your right knee... or the other way around.

Demonstrate by twisting and lifting the knee a little. If twisting right, lift the right knee.

Now try the other side, same action.

Demonstrate on the other side.

Good, let's add one other movement. As you twist left and lift the left knee, take your right elbow and tap your left knee.

Demonstrate the action of taping opposite elbow to opposite knee.

And the other side. Let's see if we can keep the action smooth and even. Remember to breathe... and keep it going... twist right and lift the right knee, take your left elbow and tap your right knee.

Demonstrate the action moving in each direction.

Keep going if this feels good... go at your own pace.

Stop when you are ready... notice how you feel... notice new sensations along the spine.

CHAPTER 8
ENERGIZING PRACTICES

Most of us have heard, or intuitively sense, that breathing a longer, deeper breath is calming to one's nervous system. However, it does not seem to be commonly understood that certain breathing and movement practices can be energizing or activating to the autonomic nervous system as well. For example, whereas extending the exhale activates the parasympathetic branch of the nervous system, prolonging the inhale activates its sympathetic branch. Energizing practices work well to help you wake up in the morning or to reinvigorate your mid-afternoon slump when your energy naturally drops. Some societies even cultivate an afternoon *siesta* time to match the body's natural inclination and rhythm. In most jobs I've had, my boss didn't appreciate my following this natural inclination to take a siesta (darn it). If you are in a similar situation, you may find the following practices quite helpful in elevating your mood and energy level.

PRACTICE 1
HORSE WHINNY

Time: 1 minute

Description: This practice is aptly named; it sounds just like a horse whinny. It is fun, expressive, and easy. The longer inhale helps energize clients by stimulating the sympathetic branch of the autonomic nervous system, followed by a comparably shorter exhale (or whinny). When introducing the practice, I usually acknowledge that it looks and sounds a bit silly. Doing so helps people loosen up a little and decreases self-consciousness or embarrassment. The movement often mirrors that of a deep sigh or a shrug—or a wordless, embodied version of "it is what it is." This is a good practice to do anytime you see excessive tension in your client's face. It also can be a good way to transition to the next part of the session.

Special Practice: If you are teaching a group and they are sitting at tables, it helps to direct clients to move away from the table so they don't hit the table. While this may seem obvious, their proprioception (sense of where they are in space in relation to other objects) may be off if they are upset or agitated.

Script

Let's try a horse whinny. It is just like it sounds and looks a little silly.
But it releases tension from the face. It is also fun. I think it sounds like
a horse whinny, but others have said it sounds more like a motorboat.
With that in mind... notice your face... is there any tension
in your jaw?... your eyes?... your cheeks?

Let's practice the sound first... inhale slowly through the nose, and then
on the exhale, purse your lips together and make a horse or motor
sound, quickly pushing the air through your pursed lips... it's
the sort of sound kids make a lot.

> *Demonstrate making the sound by inhaling through the nose and exhaling through the mouth, pursing the lips and making a whinny or motor sound. Emphasize the slow inhale and the quick exhale.*

Let's add an arm movement. Lift both hands up above your
head on the inhale, and let them flop down on the exhale.

> *Demonstrate lifting your hands up over your head and then flopping them back down to your sides.*

Yes... that's right... let's try together... slowly inhale, lifting your hands up over your head, and then quickly exhale, dropping your arms back down to your sides... okay, good.

Let's do it three times... inhale, lift... exhale, drop... inhale, lift... exhale, drop... inhale, lift... exhale, drop.

Demonstrate the movement with the sound.

Let your arms relax by your side... notice how you feel... notice your face... is there tension?... is your jaw relaxed?

PRACTICE 2
BREATH OF JOY

Time: 2 minutes

Description: Breath of joy is generally an energizing practice. I like to do it in the morning to wake myself up. You could use it the same way. Or you can use it to revitalize clients who might be low in energy after trying a quieter practice. Breath of Joy is done while standing with enough room to move your arms like a choral conductor. I have noticed that people (myself included) have a tendency to overdo or exaggerate the movements. You want the movement to be somewhere between seeming robotic and exaggerated (without hitting anything). In addition, people new to the practice sometimes put too much emphasis on the *ha* at the end of the movement and fold forward dramatically. While the *ha* can be loud and forward moving, it is also intended to be measured and thoughtful—*not* an opportunity to throw your back out.

Special Preparation: Make sure the space is clear of furniture, bookcases, and other knickknacks. There should be enough space to move your arms around.

Caution: Do not practice if you have unmedicated high blood pressure, a head or eye injury, migraines, or glaucoma (Weintraub, 2012).

Script

Let's practice Breath of Joy, a breathing practice meant
to elevate mood and lift energy.

First, let's learn the mechanics of this practice a little. You are going to
move your arms up and down, like a symphony conductor.

Lift your arms up toward the ceiling, then out to the sides,
then toward the sky, and then down toward the ground.

Good... now let's coordinate that with the breath... inhale, lift the arms
toward the sky. Exhale them out to the side. Inhale them back up, and
then exhale, bending your knees and swinging your arms down while
saying a loud ha... let's practice slowly to get the mechanics of it.

> *Demonstrate the movement. The ha sound is made by
> keeping the mouth open and breathing out forcefully
> so you can hear the actual sound ha.*

Inhale, lift the arms, exhale the arms away from the body, inhale the arms back up again, and ha while swinging the arms down... good. Now, let's do it three times on the count of three. One, two, three. Inhale, exhale, inhale, ha... inhale, exhale, inhale, ha... inhale, exhale, inhale, ha. Excellent.

Go to a natural in-and-out breath through the nose...what do you notice?... has your energy shifted?... do you need to catch your breath?

If your client is smiling...

A possible side effect of this practice is smiling.

Amanda's Story: Learning to Tolerate Physical Sensations

Amanda was a 23-year-old college graduate who began working with a colleague of mine, Dr. Bertha Jackson, to address anxiety related to her history of attachment trauma. When Amanda initially presented to therapy, she reported that her body and mind were "exhausted by anxiety." Amanda had been in a series of physically and sexually abusive dating relationships during high school and college, and she began abusing multiple legal and illegal drugs during that time to numb or "feel human."

When Dr. Jackson initially introduced breathing practices in session, such as square breathing, Amanda reported feeling overwhelmed and disconnected from her body. To meet Amanda's level of anxiety and to facilitate calm alertness of body and mind, Dr. Jackson introduced Breath of Joy at the beginning of each psychotherapy session, preceded and followed by Mountain Pose. With consistent in-session practice, Amanda began to notice and tolerate physical sensations in her body. For example, in the Mountain Pose that preceded the movement, Amanda reported feeling connected to her feet as she noticed the sensation of blood rushing to her lower extremities. She also reported the experience of "taking up space in a good way" at the end of the practice. She became increasingly aware of sensations in her arms and hands, and she was eventually able to experience this awareness as pleasant instead of overwhelming.

PRACTICE 3
BEE BREATHING

Time: 5 minutes

Description: As the name suggests, the sound of this breath is like that of a bee buzzing. Although bee breathing takes a little more time to teach and practice, I have found that it is well worth the effort. Certain added components of the breath—such as whether your lips are partially open or closed, or whether you incorporate a hand gesture—determine the intensity of the practice. The practice is designed to reduce sensory input, particularly through the eyes and ears. By closing both the eyes and ears, the *zzz* sound is intensified and reverberates in your head. It heightens your awareness inside your head without turning on your thoughts.

I have found that bee breathing has an immediate and deep calming effect, but at the same time, it is quietly energizing. It also is a breath that can interrupt obsessive and compulsive thoughts. This breath has a refreshing quality to it. One client rather poetically described its effect as: "This breath feels like splashing cool mountain water on my face… so refreshing and restorative." Introduce Bee Breathing after you have established a comfortable familiarity with simpler practices.

Script

We are going to learn Bee Breathing because it is often
a refreshing practice that can lift your energy… let's
try it and see if that rings true for you.

I am going to teach it in two parts. First, we will learn the breathing
part. Then we will learn the hand gesture part. Let's begin
by simply making a zzz sound on the exhale… inhale and….

Make the zzz sound as you exhale through your mouth.

Good… you may notice that it feels a little ticklish on
the lips as the sound vibrates the skin. Now let's
try it with the lips slightly apart. Like this…

Make the zzz sound on the exhale with your lips closer together.

Notice the breath goes from sounding like one bee
to a hive of bees… let's try it once again.

Make the zzz sound on the exhale with your lips closed.

Now we are ready to practice the hand gesture.
Put your hands on your head like a helmet.

Demonstrate putting your hands on your head.

Let's try it together. I will provide cueing to set us up. When we are ready to go, we will do three rounds of zzzs. Since your exhale will be different, when you are done with your three, place your hands in your lap… any questions so far?

Make the zzz sound three times while your hands are on your head. Keep your eyes open so you can "peek" at your client or the group. When you notice they are on their third zzz, place your hands in your lap.

When you are finished with your third zzz… taking all the time you need… relax your hands in your lap.

Notice when their hands are in their lap.

Sense your right hand, sense your left hand, sense your right foot, sense your left foot. Perhaps you notice the glow of the honeybee… open your eyes if they are still closed.

Notice what expression you see.

Notice what you notice… if you have one or two words to describe your experience of this breath… you may share it now if you want to.

Sharing is completely optional. Sitting in silence for a minute or two may also be an appropriate choice.

PRACTICE 4
HALF SALUTE

Time: 5 minutes

Description: Generally speaking, a practice like the Half Salute—which activates the large muscle groups as you bend your knees, sweep your arms overhead, and fold your body forward—is energizing and helps the blood circulate. At the same time, the movement is slow and thoughtful. I often offer a series of half salutes at the beginning of a session in order to help clients feel grounded and centered.

When this practice becomes familiar to you, the simple rhythmic movement will lend itself well to the addition of affirmations or a prayer. But it can be too much for many people to take in at once if you teach new movements with the words. The idea is to be present with any sensations that arise in the body. If clients need to think about or remember new words at the same time, one action tends to compromise the other. This may sound surprising because neither the movement nor the affirmation is necessarily complex. I think the challenge arises from our cultural deconditioning of not regularly moving our bodies or joints within their range of motion each day. It becomes easy to forget that the body has a bigger role than simply carrying around our head and brain all day.

If you haven't been moving much and you start doing this practice daily for even five minutes, you will feel it. Receive this felt sense of your body as encouragement. *I can feel my body as a result of consistent, mindful movement. This is good.* And try not to overdo it. Stopping before you feel fatigued is key.

Special Preparation: The Half Salute is a very handy practice because it can be done while standing or sitting, and it can be done without a yoga mat and without prior knowledge of yoga. Given that the practice involves sweeping the arms out wide, make sure that there is ample room to do so.

Script

Standing Version:

Let's check in with how your body is feeling in this moment... notice the pace of your breathing.

The half salute involves some sweeping arm actions and big body movements... let me demonstrate the movement... it begins with inhaling the arms up to the sky... exhaling and hinging at the hips and reaching down... inhaling up halfway, like an L shape... exhaling down into forward fold… inhaling all the way back up, pressing through the feet… it's okay to bend the knees here… sweeping the arms wide and bringing them back to heart center.

Demonstrate the movement.

Let's try it together… inhale… sweep the arms up… exhale… hinge forward into forward fold… inhale, come up halfway… exhale… forward fold… inhale, press your feet into the floor to come up… sweep the arms up… then exhale… hands returning to heart center.

Cue with words and now watch their movement.

Let's try it together… inhale… sweep the arms up… exhale… hinge forward into forward fold… inhale, come up halfway… exhale… forward fold… inhale, press your feet into the floor to come up… sweep the arms up… then exhale… hands returning to heart center.

Soften your face… notice how you feel… do you want to do a few more, or is this a good resting place?

Seated Variation:

Let's check in with how your body is feeling in this moment… as you sit comfortably in your chair, notice the pace of your breathing.

The seated half salute involves some sweeping arm actions and big body movements… let me demonstrate the movement… it begins with inhaling the arms up to the sky… exhaling and hinging at the hips and reaching down while sitting… inhaling up halfway… exhaling and folding forward in your chair… inhaling all the way back up, pressing your feet into the floor… sweeping the arms wide and bringing them back to heart center.

If you are unable to hinge forward… you can lift one knee toward your chest… using your hands under the knee to support the movement… then place your foot back on the floor and bring the other knee toward your chest… again using your hands under your knee to aid in the movement… and then returning that foot to the floor.

Demonstrate the movement.

Let's try it together… inhale… sweep the arms up… exhale… hinge forward into forward fold… inhale, come up halfway… exhale… forward fold… inhale, press your feet into the floor to come up… sweep the arms up… then exhale… hands returning to heart center.

Cue with words and now watch their movement.

Let's try it together… inhale… sweep the arms up… exhale… hinge forward into forward fold… inhale, come up halfway… exhale… forward fold… inhale, press your feet into the floor to come up… sweep the arms up… then exhale… hands returning to heart center.

Soften your face… notice how you feel… do you want to do a few more, or is this a good resting place?

PRACTICE 5

BELLOW'S BREATH

Time: 3-4 minutes

Description: Bellow's Breath is aptly named after the old-fashioned handheld fireplace bellow used to add more oxygen to the fire. Along these same lines, Bellow's Breath pulls oxygen into your body. The forceful breath, along with the pumping arm action, acts as a distribution system that allows lymph to move around the body. We want lymph to move around our body, just as we want blood to circulate throughout our body. However, the blood has a pump to perform this function (the heart), whereas lymph does not. By pumping the arms gently above the head, you can activate lymph flow by stimulating the major lymph nodes in the armpits. This is a good thing because lymph is like a vacuum cleaner for the body. It helps remove toxins and unwanted debris, which supports a healthy immune system.

In this practice, the arm actions are coupled with a breath that sounds a bit like a freight train. The mouth is closed, and the nose performs both a quick inhale that sucks the diaphragm in and a short snapping exhale that pushes the diaphragm out. A typical response to this breath is an increase in energy. I liken the effect to that of drinking a cup of coffee, except without the jitters or having to pay four bucks at a coffee shop. After doing this practice, you may even want to take your pulse. It may be elevated. This is good information to note in case you are in need of a practice to naturally elevate your mood and energy.

I typically introduce this practice toward the end of a session. If a client is new to breathing practices, they may feel a little lightheaded at first. This is not unusual; it is simply the body's response to the newness of a rapid breath. Any normal lightheadedness will generally dissipate in a minute or two. However, I suggest introducing this practice after clients have mastered simpler practices, like nasal breathing.

Caution: Do not practice if you have unmedicated high blood pressure or shoulder issues (Weintraub, 2012).

Script

This practice has two parts: the breathing part and the arm movement part. Let's start with the arm movements. Hold your hands open in front of you with your palms up, and curl your fingers over your thumbs. Now raise your arms straight up to the ceiling and then back down to shoulder level. The speed is about one second up and one second down. Or perhaps a little faster, just not a rapid-fire movement.

Let's try adding the breath… with your hands in fists at shoulder level, inhale the hands up and exhale them down. Now let's make the breath a short inhale through the nose and a forceful exhale through nose.

Demonstrate the inhale and exhale.

Use about the same amount of force as you would use to blow out birthday candles, except your air is coming out of the nose. Inhale, exhale. Now let's put the arm action and the breathing together. Make fists, ready at shoulder height. Inhale, arms up. Exhale, arms down.

Demonstrate the arm action with the arms going up on the inhale and returning to shoulder level on the exhale.

Good. Now that you've got the mechanics of it down, let's try about ten… beginning on the count of three. One, two, three, inhale, exhale.

Repeat ten times at the pace of one second for each inhale and exhale.

Good, now let's do two slow ones. Inhale, exhale, inhale, exhale. Let your hands relax, breathing naturally.

Notice how you feel.

Sense into your right hand… sense into your left hand… sense into your right foot… sense into your left foot… notice your whole body.

PRACTICE 6
UPPER BODY JOINT ROTATION

Time: 3-4 minutes

Description: Moving our joints systematically each day allows the synovial fluid to lubricate the joints. This fluid is already in your body, but it requires movement on your part to be activated. The body doesn't need much time, space, or complexity of movement to perform this activation. This practice, which was inspired by Mukunda Stiles's *Joint Freeing Series* (2002), can occur at the beginning of a session or whenever it feels like a good time to move the body. Stiffness and immobility impact our mood, and loosening the joints in this gentle, practical way will most likely have positive effects on mood. We are sometimes not even aware that we are stiff until we start moving our body and joints in this intentional way.

Special Preparation: If you'd like, you can play some calming instrumental music as a backdrop.

Script

Your body is truly amazing. It has a built-in system to lubricate the joints. Every day, we need to move each joint through its pain-free range of motion to release the synovial fluid to juice the joints. Let's try rotating your joints. Make sure you are sitting up straight in your chair... with your feet on the ground... hip-width apart... your spine is straight... and your chest is lifted slightly in Chair Mountain.

Notice the texture of your breath... is it smooth?... or is it ragged?... can you slow it down just a little?

Let's start with the hands and wrists... with your hands in front of your chest and your elbows bent, start circling the wrists.

What are you noticing?

Spread out the fingers of each hand a few times... like stars... and circle your wrists back in the other direction.

Demonstrate circling the wrists and making stars with the hands.

Now move your hands around like you are conducting an orchestra. Involve the wrists and elbows.

Demonstrate elbow and finger/arm movements.

Soften your face... breathe.

Keep conducting your imaginary orchestra, gradually exaggerating your movements so your shoulders are now moving along with your elbows and wrists. Perhaps one arm moves a little more easily than the other.

Demonstrate the previous movement in a more exaggerated way so your arms and shoulders are moving and the arm bones are moving in their sockets.

Notice how your body feels… check-in with your breath.

PRACTICE 7

LOWER BODY JOINT ROTATION

Time: 3-5 minutes

Description: Like the Upper Body Joint Rotation, the Lower Body Joint Rotation is about moving the joints of the lower body in their full range-of-motion. This includes ankles, knees, and hips. Also like the Upper Body Joint Rotation, this practice is inspired by the Mukunda Stiles's *Joint Freeing Series* (2002). The practice is simple and accessible from the chair. Hip mobility is very important for one's daily routine such as getting bathed and dressed. Synovial fluid is released into the joints as they rotate and/or hinge (depending on which joint), hence facilitating the lubrication of the joint and ease of movement. Take your time and don't rush through the practice. This practice can be done anytime during a session, but I most often use it early on in a session to help a client feel more grounded and present in their body.

Special Preparation: If you'd like, you can play some calming instrumental music as a backdrop.

Script

Let's focus on the joints in the lower half of the body…knees,
ankles, and hips… notice how your body feels right
now in this moment… find your breath.

Lift one knee… then place it back down… lift the other
knee… then place it back down… good… Repeat.

Demonstrate the movement.

Lift one knee and rotate the ankle in mid-air… nice… now
rotate in the other direction… try some pointing and flexing
of that foot. Your hands can help to hold up your leg.

Return your foot to the floor, and lift the other
foot a few inches off the floor.

Rotate the ankle… nice… now rotate in the other direction…
try some pointing and flexing of that foot… send some love
to your feet… that is not something we are in the habit of
doing—saying love and feet in the same sentence.

Lifting the other knee… we are going to rotate the hip…
the deepest ball-and-socket joint… moving the head of the
femur in the hip socket… good… now change directions.
It will look like your knee is making a little circle.

Now adding a little external rotation… place the outer side of your foot
on your opposite knee… if it goes there easily… if not, put it on your
shin. Keep breathing… imagine your breath is going into the
space you have created from externally rotating your hip.

Demonstrate the action. Stay here for several breaths.

Uncrossing your leg and lifting up the other knee… we are going to rotate
the hip on the other side… notice if this one feels different
than on the other side… now change directions.

Now on the other side… yes, what we do on one side, we get to do on
the other side to even ourselves out… put the outer side of your foot
on your knee… and breathe… or place it on your shin… whichever feels
easier and allows you to breathe smoothly… again, keep breathing…
imagine your breath is going into the space you have created.

Uncross your leg… with both feet on the floor… notice how you feel.

PRACTICE 8
SHAKING

Time: 3-6 minutes

Description: The practice of shaking helps to circulate blood and lymph in the body and has an overall effect of elevating mood and energy levels. The practice is more energetic than you may initially think, and it will require your focused attention and sustained movement in your pain-free range of motion. Start small with your hands and feet. If you are standing, you obviously will not be able to shake both feet at once. It may feel awkward as you work your way through the process of shaking the legs, hips, torso, and shoulders. But the movements get smoother and more comfortable with practice. This shaking practice should be done very gently, and I recommend starting out for about three minutes when you try it the first few times. This is a favorite practice among young adults I teach. They appreciate the awake and alert feeling they get from the practice. At the same time, I have witnessed older veterans successfully doing this practice from a chair and enjoying it. It is a fun practice to do early in a session if a client has low energy.

Special Preparation: Although this practice can be done sitting, it is more effective when done standing (if this is possible given your client's physical abilities and the space you have available). I often use music for this practice, although I am careful not to choose songs with too many beats per minute. I want to encourage slow and gentle movement, not fast movement.

Script

Whether you are sitting or standing, start by noticing your breathing…
where are you noticing your breath in your body?

Can you transition to a slow, even breath?…
perhaps you are there already.

Once we achieve that slow, even breath, we can begin. Start by
gently shaking your hands and wiggling your fingers… get the
elbows involved. We are going for a jiggling effect. Eventually,
we will move every body part that is able to move.

Demonstrate gently shaking the hands and fingers, then the elbows.

If it all feels like too much, just do one body part at a time.

Demonstrate shaking one hand at a time.

Start to shake your shoulders… if you can. If not, move
on to your torso… and then your hips.

Demonstrate gently shaking the shoulders, torso, and hips.

Begin shaking your legs… knees… feet. Pause if you are starting to overdo it… no pain… no throwing your back out… that wouldn't look good for either of us.

Now that you've gotten your groove going, see what you can sustain for a few minutes… perhaps it will be just your hands and arms with an occasional shoulder shimmy… or maybe you want to focus on your legs and knees.

Watch for fatigue. Encourage pausing. Look for a natural stopping point. Keeping shaking for at least four minutes.

Allow yourself to come to stillness… what is your breath doing?… how is your body feeling?… is there one word that characterizes how you feel right now? Feel free to share it.

Make a mental note to yourself—in which pocket of my toolbelt does this practice belong?

PRACTICE 9
LION'S BREATH

Time: 2 minutes

Description: Lion's Breath is fun, powerful, and energizing for most people. Since this breath involves poking the tongue out, it gives me permission to do something that doesn't fit so well in other parts of my life. Now that you are intrigued, let's try it out. You could use this energizer for yourself when you are between client sessions or with a client if you notice that they come into a session with low energy. It is also a good practice to use to help someone find their voice. Additionally, Lion's Breath can release tension in the face and throat.

Script

Lion's Breath is an easy way to energize yourself and release
upper body tension… this breath is done from Chair Mountain.
But first, let's check in with your body… is there any tension
in your face?… if there is, release it if you can.

Begin with your hands resting on your thighs… find your breath…
open your eyes wide, look up, and on the next inhale… with a
straight spine, lift your hands in front of your chest, spreading
the fingers wide like stars… and exhale… making a fairly
forceful ha sound while sticking your tongue out.

*Demonstrate placing your hands on your thighs, looking up, inhaling,
and exhaling ha. The ha is breathy rather than a forceful sound.*

Now don't be shy… I know it looks a little silly… but we can
be silly together… it's a great tension releaser.

Let your hands rest comfortably on your thighs… find your breath…
open your eyes wide, look up, and on the next inhale… lift your
chest and hands, like stars, and exhale ha… tongue poking out.

And again… open your eyes wide, look up, and on the next inhale…
lift your chest and hands, like stars, and exhale ha.

Relax your body and your face… notice how you feel.

CHAPTER 9

VISUALIZATIONS AND MEDITATIONS

Using our imagination to visualize something does not come easily to many of us. But the good news is that visualizing is a skill that can be learned and developed. When introducing these visualization exercises, I have found that most people are open to very simple visualizations where they allow their thoughts to gather around the images being visualized instead of ruminating on their own thoughts. I have made the following practices quite short in order to keep them accessible and to help your clients feel successful with this aspect of the practice.

The following visualizations are also a form of meditation. However, be aware that some people are uncomfortable with the word *meditation* itself because they associate it with a religious practice and do not consider themselves religious. On the other hand, I have had many people light up when they hear the word *meditation* and say, "I've always wanted to learn to meditate." I recommend finding out a person's comfort level with the word and the practice. This information helps to inform the practice and provide a framework that makes sense to them. The practices I have included in this chapter are secular in nature and do not require a particular belief system. By helping clients cultivate a meditation practice, you can facilitate mindful awareness and self-awareness, which is one of the foundational principles undergirding all the practices.

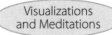

PRACTICE 1
AWARENESS MEDITATION

Time: 3-5 minutes

Description: In this meditation practice, you use the sounds in your environment to ground you in the present moment. By noticing what you hear and then releasing it, it helps slow the mind. And once the mind has quieted, you can more easily identify and differentiate between your thoughts.

The act of noticing is a useful skill to cultivate, and it is sometimes known as metacognition, or thinking about thinking. The process helps you to differentiate between your thoughts and allows you to realize that you are more than the sum total of your thoughts. You can liken the mind to a canoe floating down a quiet stream. Although the stream is quiet, it can unexpectedly turn into a whitewater rapid at the blink of an eye. Our mind takes us places. Sometimes this is welcome, sometimes it is not.

This awareness meditation can be done at the beginning or end of a session. It also offers a way to practice meditation even at a busy place, like an airport. If someone announces that their mind is racing or scattered, or they tell you they are "all over the place," then having them take even three to five minutes to notice what their mind is doing—without engaging or responding to their thoughts—can be helpful. It can also be helpful for them to simply realize that their mind seems rather busy today. Watch for body language. Are they fidgety? Is their breathing shallow? If so, these clues suggest that you do a shorter practice. Less is more.

Special Preparation: Sitting in a chair is best. You will also need a timer. If you use the timer on your phone, make sure that you first explain to your client why your phone is visible.

Script

This practice is about being aware of your thoughts. Begin by noticing
the speed and quality of your thoughts… are they busy and fast?...
Quiet and slow?… or maybe anxious and frazzled?

Let yourself be comfortable in your seat… choose to have your
eyes open or closed… notice the sound of your breath…
Watch the movement of your breath.

Notice the sounds that you hear right now… notice a sound outside the
room… notice a sound inside the room, even if it is just the silence.

Now notice the next thought that arises… don't judge it
or engage it… just notice that it is a thought.

Let it go by moving on to the next thought, and then return to the sound of your breath.

Each time you notice a sound or thought... pause... notice... don't judge or evaluate.

Return your attention to your breath... Continue to notice sounds and thoughts without judgment for the next minute or so. I will keep time so you don't need to. I will bring this exercise to a close in about two minutes.

I am here with you, collecting sounds in silence, watching my thoughts as well.

Keep time as you said you would, perhaps two to four minutes.

Bring your awareness back to the sounds in the room... notice the hum of the room... notice the absence of sound in the room... if your eyes are closed... open them.

Orient yourself to the room. Notice the color of the walls. Notice where the wall meets the ceiling.

Notice the sound of your breath... notice the speed and quality of your thoughts right now... how you are feeling?

PRACTICE 2
HAND ON HEART, HAND ON BELLY

Time: 5 minutes

Description: This practice is a good way to begin cultivating a small act of compassion for yourself. It involves placing your hands on your own body, which allows for a more tactile experience with the body. There is a whole category of gestures in yoga called *mudras* that have different meanings and effects. For example, placing one hand on your belly and one on your heart is commonly accepted as a kind gesture toward oneself. I often offer this practice toward the end of a session, or as the closing practice of the session, thereby culminating in a heartfelt and visceral gesture of self-compassion. Gently guiding clients along the journey from self-loathing to self-love can be a long one. It is small, simple, and accessible practices like this one that can nudge your client along the path.

This practice can arouse a surprising amount of emotion. Don't be surprised if you find yourself becoming emotional as you say the words, even the scripted ones. Because this practice is so powerful, you will need to feel up to the task of emotionally holding the space and ensuring that your pacing and tone of voice is authentically caring and soothing. Be sure to speak slowly and earnestly. There is a good chance your client is going to hear these words only from you today, so your words and tone matter. Mean them; embody the words. Otherwise, don't do this meditation. It's better to skip it if you can't be entirely present and to save it for another day. As with all the practices, being able to do the practice for yourself first is key.

Special Preparation: I usually use soft, slow instrumental music (sixty to eighty beats per minute) as background. The feedback from clients is nearly always positive. If you do a Google or YouTube search, you will find examples of this type of music.

Script

We are going to spend a few minutes visualizing and developing awareness of our bodies… Please join me if you would like to try it… if not, feel free to observe quietly.

Place one hand on your heart and one hand on your belly… feel their weight… and warmth… and kindness… your eyes can be open or closed, whichever you prefer.

Demonstrate the gesture.

Take a moment and notice this gesture... it's often a gesture of comfort or wholeheartedness... and that's what we are communicating nonverbally to ourselves right now.

These gestures are for you... a way for you to comfort and care for yourself... yes, even caring for ourselves requires practice... and we know we get better at things we practice.

Recognize that your heart is beating under your hand... perhaps you can feel the beating of your heart.

Don't worry if you can't... we have to be in a pretty still and quiet place to feel that... but even if you don't... simply sense the work of your heart... since it works on your behalf... even without you thinking about it... it is one of the many automatic functions of your amazing body.

Just know that being here right now... your heart is doing its job.

As you hold your hand over your heart... see your heart in your mind's eye... pumping... working hard... taking care of business for you... moment by moment.

It is okay to close the eyes for a few seconds and to encourage clients to close theirs if they want to. But, for the most part, your eyes should be open. Watch your clients with a soft gaze so they don't feel like you are staring at them intently.

Be aware of this inner working... the heart steadily beating under your hand.

Bring to mind something or someone for which (or for whom) you feel a deep sense of gratitude.

If you notice gratitude arising... go with it... but if you don't, that's fine... don't feel as if you have to manufacture something... just stay with the beating of your heart... recognizing its life-giving force.

What we are doing right now is the essence of self-awareness... notice your breathing... in and out.

Now shift your awareness... that just means noticing... to your belly and the hand on your belly... what do you sense?

Sometimes our breathing is deep enough to move the belly…
if you don't feel your breath and your belly going up and
down gently… then try breathing a little deeper if you
can… breathe in and out through your nose.

Notice your belly… perhaps it is moving now… this deep,
slow breath is a particular way to care for yourself.

Our ability to care for ourselves is vital to our well-being… it
is vital that we take the time to acknowledge that caring
for ourselves and being aware of ourselves are two
vital aspects of robust physical and mental health.

And that's what you are doing for yourself right now… in
this moment… being aware of and caring for yourself…
notice how it feels to do this for yourself.

No one can do this work for you… Only you can do it for yourself.

Perhaps remain still and quiet for a minute or so.

In a few moments, let your hands relax by your sides… notice the
absence of your hands from your body… the change of pressure.

Remember your hands' capacity for kindness… are there
other people to whom these hands can be kind?

You have just practiced self-care and self-awareness…
congratulate yourself… notice how it feels.

PRACTICE 3
TENSE AND RELAX

Time: 3-4 minutes

Description: Sometimes our body forgets that there is a difference between tense muscles and relaxed muscles. Doing this simple tense-and-relax exercise can help your body remember the difference. Tension will often dissipate when you realize it is there. Help yourself or your client identify where the tension is before it gets worse or chronic in nature. Although this practice usually relaxes the body—and could therefore have been included with the calming practices—I tend to see it as both a visualization and a meditation. In its simplicity, it can be done anywhere, anytime. Though the act of tensing and relaxing the muscles is a physical action (and the intention is indeed to tense and relax the muscles), in the early stages of practicing, it may be more doable for clients to visualize their muscles tensing and relaxing.

It is important not to rush this practice, which is another reason why I see it as a meditation. Notice whether your client is following along by observing whether they are tensing and relaxing the body parts as you name them. Do less if they are not tracking with you. Doing this practice even with just a few body parts can be enough to remind your body of the difference between tense and relaxed states. You can offer this practice at the beginning or end of the session. You can also suggest it whenever a client seems tense or you are aware of tension in your own body.

Script

This practice will help remind your body of the difference between being tense and relaxed. Before we begin, simply notice your body in this moment… perhaps you are aware of tension… just notice it and name it if you can… notice if your breathing is fast or slow.

This practice is exactly as it sounds. We are going to tense and relax various muscles. Don't worry if you are unable to tense and relax a particular part of your body. Over time, it will become easier to tense and relax isolated muscles at will.

For now, just go with what you can do today. Bring your awareness to each part of the body I name, and see if you can contract or tighten the related muscles or make them tense. We will hold the contracted muscles for a few seconds and then release.

Let's start with something nice and simple… make a fist or two and then release… and again… and release.

Demonstrate each action if you can.

Now bring your awareness to the top of your
head... tense... hold and relax.

Now the eyes and mouth. Pucker up your face like
you are sucking on lemons... tense... hold and relax.

The jaw... tense... hold and relax.

The shoulders... hunch them up... tense... hold and relax.

The arms... tense... hold and relax.

The chest and belly... tense... hold and relax.

The buttocks... tense... hold and relax.

The thighs... tense... hold and relax.

The feet and toes... tense... hold and relax.

Returning to your face... run your tongue over your
teeth... purse your lips... and release.

Now notice your breath... scan for tension in your
body... what do you notice?

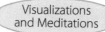
PRACTICE 4
I AM HERE NOW

Time: 3-4 minutes

Description: First-person, present-tense affirmations can ground you and support you in being present in the moment—instead of mentally checking out. In this practice, you will practice pairing an affirmation with an accompanying hand gesture. Coordinating hand gestures and words can sometimes be surprisingly challenging. This practice can be done anytime during the session, but it is particularly helpful if you notice that you or your client are dissociating. Start the practice quietly. It is fine to increase the volume as you get used to saying the words combined with the hand gestures. Avoid simply going on autopilot. The purpose of this practice is to help you be in the present moment. It can serve as a reminder to be in the here and now.

Script

This practice involves repeating a phrase to yourself (an affirmation) and linking it with a hand gesture. The sensation of pressing your fingers together and linking this movement to words can help orient you to the present moment.

Let's start by noticing how you are feeling right now... take your awareness to your hands... how do they feel? With each hand, touch your thumb to the tip of your index finger. Then touch your thumb to the tip of your middle finger, then to your ring finger, and finally to your pinky finger.

Demonstrate the finger actions.

To repeat the movement, go back to touching
your thumb to your index finger.

Let's practice... index... middle... ring and pinky... good.

Demonstrate the finger movements.

Now let's add the affirmation... "I am here now"...
Four words, four fingers.

You got it... they go together.

Demonstrate combining the finger movements to the words.

I am here now. You can say it out loud or silently to yourself...
repeat three times along with the hand gestures. I am here
now... I am here now... I am here now.

Relax your hands... notice how you feel.

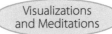

PRACTICE 5
COLOR INFUSION

Time: 4-5 minutes

Description: This practice involves using a color to describe what is going on internally, even when we don't have words for our feelings. I have found it to be a useful tool to identify and express emotion. There are no right or wrong colors to choose. This practice allows clients to begin learning how to differentiate between emotions before they actually have the words to do so. I tend to practice this exercise more with children, who seem to intuitively identify colors to describe their current feelings. You could introduce this practice early in a session, although I often do it at the end. That way, clients take their color with them when they leave. I explain that I am going to give them a color—a color of their choosing. The color often mirrors their mood, but not always. Whatever color they choose is just fine.

Special Preparation: When working in a group context, this practice can be done with clients seated in chairs. If I am doing this with a group, I will sometimes play Kira Willey's song *Colors* as a backdrop. Be sure to allow enough time to give everyone a color. It's fine for more than one person in the group to have the same color. If you are using this practice in an individual session, you can invite clients to lie down on a yoga mat or to sit in a chair.

Script

Today, I am going to give you a color to leave with… it can
be any color you choose… it may be your favorite color,
or it can simply be a color you like or feel like today.

Take a moment and tune in to yourself… notice how you
are feeling right now… does a color come to mind?

Just pick the first one that pops into your mind… sometimes
our color reflects our mood in some way.

We are going to use our imagination to choose our color… here's what
it will look like… I will stand in front of you and say, "What color would
you like today?" You will tell me your color… this is how I give you your
color… I will pantomime tapping on your shoulders without actually
touching you… then you will hear me go whoosh and say, "Here's your
color." I will pantomime painting your color on you without actually
touching you. If doing this in a group setting, add: Then I will
move on to the next person until everyone has a color.

Remember to just pick the first color that pops into your mind.

Cue your music and begin. Ask what color they want. Give it to them with a little whoosh sound. Continue until everyone has a color.

Now you have a color… let your color settle… all over you.

You can take your color with you… how does your color feel?… do you notice your color in a particular place in your body?

Notice how you feel.

PRACTICE 6
WHAT DOES GRATITUDE LOOK LIKE?

Time: 3 minutes

Description: The practice of gratitude is not about looking for a silver lining in every circumstance or about the power of positive thinking, although it could involve either. It is about pausing and noticing something we are grateful for in any given day, hour, or moment. When we cultivate gratitude, and even savor it, gratitude builds upon itself. We are better humans when we give thanks. Gratitude is not simply an attitude; it is a practice. It is the antidote to "foreboding joy," which is when something good happens but we can't fully take it in because there is a sense that it can't possibly last, as if we are waiting for the other shoe to drop (Brown, 2018). A gratitude practice allows for real joy to settle in.

Just because this is a gratitude exercise doesn't automatically mean clients will be overwhelmed with a feeling of gratitude. But eventually the feeling of gratitude will arise. I remind people that they don't have to try to manufacture any feeling. If it occurs, great. If it doesn't, then the act of naming something they are grateful for is enough. It is a powerful exercise. This practice can be done anytime during a group or individual session. It can also be an opening or closing ritual.

Special Preparation: You may want to have some soft instrumental music playing in the background as you practice this exercise. I try to have the music be as neutral as possible, as opposed to using musical pieces that are easily recognizable, such as *Canon in D*. The music is literally acting as a backdrop for the practice. Try it with and without music, and see which you prefer.

Script

Let's take a moment to connect to our breath.

The purpose of this practice is to tune in and notice what
we are grateful for… when we do this practice of gratitude…
even for a few minutes daily… we start to find ourselves
cultivating a habit of being grateful.

Very gently, notice what arises within you… any
initial thoughts… feelings… simply notice them.

Place your hand on your heart… the symbol of our emotional center…
with your eyes open and gaze softened, or eyes closed … whichever
is more comfortable to you… see in your mind's eye something
or someone that you are deeply grateful for… past or present.

Try to see your person or object in as much detail
as your imagination will allow.

Give about ten to fifteen seconds of silence here. It will seem like a lot.

Allow yourself to be with the image.

Allow for a little more silence.

Notice if the feeling of gratitude wells up… if it does, make room for it…
but don't feel like you have to force it or make yourself feel grateful.

Just stay with your image… notice your body… do
you notice any sensations?

Be with yourself for a moment… release the image…
notice how you feel.

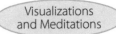
PRACTICE 7
INNER SPEEDWAY

Time: 5 minutes

Description: Somewhere, somehow, we have received cultural messages repeatedly telling us that packing as much as possible into each day is good and productive. For many of us, going fast and hurrying through life has become our modus operandi. Certainly, this was my way of life for a very long time. Going fast made me feel good about myself, or so I thought. In reality, I used perpetual movement as a crutch to avoid feeling difficult emotions, such as sadness, loss, disappointment, and grief. However, we need to learn how to make room for all our feelings, even the difficult ones, if we want to find healthy ways to acknowledge and express them. In my own experience with slowing down, I eventually came to understand that I was more than my feelings and that all my feelings were important to my human experience.

This short-guided meditation will help you connect to your inner speedway and slow down the pace of the race. As you practice noticing your inner pace, you will get better at slowing it down if you want to. Sometimes coming to the realization that you have been zooming around—and that you can slow down and *still* accomplish an acceptable number of things in a day—can be a lovely revelation. An ideal time to do this practice is when you notice that you are revved up internally and would like to slow things down. It can also be a nice practice at the end of a session.

Script

Sitting comfortably in your seat… back straight… chest lifted… feet on the floor, about hip-width apart… gaze at the back of your eyelids if you want. It is often easier to do this practice with your eyes closed. If closing your eyes is not comfortable for you today, simply soften your gaze and find a focal point in the middle of the floor.

This practice is about noticing your inner speed and slowing it down. Sometimes, even when we can move slowly on the outside, we are speeding along on the inside.

Start to notice your breathing… what is the length of your breath?

Now imagine you are a car traveling down a highway… notice what sort of car you are… if you own a car, maybe it is a car like that… or maybe it is your dream car… how fast do you think you are going?… now look at your car's dashboard… what is the speedometer telling you?… Note the speed… how does it feel?

Allow about three to five seconds of silence.

What would it feel like to go ten miles per hour
slower?... how does that feel?

Allow about three to five seconds of silence.

What about twenty miles per hour slower?... how does that feel?

Allow about three to five seconds of silence.

What about slowing down to half speed?... how does that feel?

Allow about three to five seconds of silence.

Can you slow down even more?... what are you noticing
at this new, slow pace?

Allow about three to five seconds of silence.

Now increase your speed to a pace that feels comfortable for you...
consider maintaining this speed for the rest of your trip.

Allow about three to five seconds of silence.

Start slowing down again... you are nearly at your destination...
you are just a few blocks from home... you see your driveway.

You pull up to your door.

Notice how it feels to have taken a leisurely drive home... Was
it your usual pace?... was it annoying or freeing to slow down?

Notice how you feel now.

PRACTICE 8
COOL YOUR SOUP

Time: 2-3 minutes

Description: This breathing practice involves evoking the pleasant sensations and images associated with holding and sipping a mug of hot soup on a cold day. It involves cupping the hands and blowing on the soup to cool it off. This practice is particularly handy if you or your client are having trouble connecting to, or noticing, your breath. Children like this practice too, though hot cocoa may be a little more inviting to their sensibilities.

Many of the practices in this book build on themselves. Once you have one or two practices in each pocket of your toolbelt, it becomes easier to try another three or four. I find that curiosity to explore other practices builds over time.

Script

Sitting up tall in your chair... notice your feet on the
ground... notice your bottom on the chair.

We are going to try a simple breathing practice called Cool Your Soup.

It will require a little imagination and playfulness on your part...
first, let's think of your favorite soup, if you have one.

If you want to close your eyes, that's fine... take a moment to
identify the soup... the ingredients in the soup, or at least the
main ones you can see... if the soup is homemade... see yourself
making the soup, or someone making the soup... just for
you, even if you don't know who they are.

You can stir the soup if you want. Let's be the spoon. Your whole
upper body is the spoon stirring the pot... gently and slowly.

Demonstrate making a circle with your upper body in one direction.

Good... notice whether or not it is easy to stir the
pot... now change direction.

Demonstrate making a circle in the other direction.

You can always stop if you bump up against any tender spots.

The soup is now ready. See yourself ladling it into a big mug...
you pick up the mug and cradle it in your hands.

> **Demonstrate the action of holding a large, hot mug of soup.**

Now lift the mug up to your lips and gently blow on the hot liquid… perhaps three or four times.

> **Demonstrate bringing the mug to your lips and gently blowing on the soup.**

Now take a sip… Sipping on the inhale, and then exhaling through the mouth… Mmm… show your appreciation… inhale slowly… and exhale.

> **Demonstrate sipping the soup on the inhale, then exhaling through the mouth.**

Do you taste it?… what are you noticing?

Try it a few more times… inhale… exhale… inhale… exhale.

Place your soup down, let your hands relax… notice how you feel.

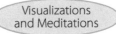

PRACTICE 9

THE TREE AND ME

Time: 5-7 minutes

Description: If nature is already a grounding place for you, then this guided imagery exercise of a tall, strong tree may also be grounding for you. I love all trees, but I am particularly fond of redwoods. There is something about their age, grandeur, and presence that feels sacred. Several years ago, I heard there was a name for the practice of spending time in nature that sounded intuitive to me. The practice originated in Japan and is known as *shinrin-yoku*, which literally translates to "forest bathing." While this practice is not literally about taking a bath, it is about slowing down and immersing yourself in nature. Although I live in a decently sized city in an urban neighborhood, I feel very fortunate that Pittsburgh is lushly green in the summer. Trees are abundant. I like to talk to them. Do you? You can use this practice to wrap up a session or at any other time that feels like a good fit.

Script

This visualization is about trees... big, strong, solid trees. So get comfortable in your chair. It may be easier to close your eyes, but if that's not comfortable, just soften your gaze... the following story is inspired by my love of trees... settle in and let yourself wander.

It is a warm, sunny day in a huge meadow on a hill... see yourself... if you want, somewhere in the meadow.

You feel the breeze on your face... take a few gulps of fresh air... it feels so good to be outside enjoying the day.

In the distance, a little way down the hill... you see a path. You follow the path toward a large expanse of trees... and the path disappears into the forest.

You hesitate for a moment... but you feel compelled by the beauty of the tall trees to enter into the forest... so you do.

It is cooler in the forest... you can no longer see sun and blue sky... instead, there is a canopy of emerald green... and the smell is... earthy and fresh... you can't quite decide what it smells like... but it is pleasant... you take in the fragrance of the forest by breathing deeply.

You look ahead. The trees all look similar to you as they stand silently at attention... as if keeping watch.

Then you see it... deep under the canopy is a much larger
tree than the ones around it... you are curious... it
is almost as if the tree is beckoning to you.

You approach carefully... not wanting to make noise
for some reason... the stillness feels holy and
beautiful... you take in the silence and let it fill you.

The stillness fills your senses with its nothingness... at first... it feels
really odd... since much of your life is noisy by comparison.

But this stillness feels calm and inviting... like
balm to your overstimulated senses.

You reach the tree and lean into its ancient barky trunk
for support... you feel its solidness.

Then you notice, in the crevice at the base of the trunk, a
small wooden box that appears to be overflowing with small pieces of
paper and sticky notes. You wonder if someone has dropped it.

You move closer to examine the box... you see a tiny sign... it says...
"Leave your troubles here, lighten your burden." You realize
what you are looking at... the small box has people's troubles
written on it, which is probably why it is so full.

You muse to yourself that you must not be the only one with troubles.

You look around, but you see no one... "What could it hurt?" you think...
and right then and there at the foot of the tree... you begin
hunting through your pockets to find a paper and pen.

You find them and start unburdening yourself,
writing down your troubles.

Allow about three to five seconds of silence.

You look around again... and still you are alone...
but you don't feel alone anymore.

You add your paper to the little box.

Standing back... you thank the tree... it probably didn't happen... but
for a second... you thought you heard, "You're welcome."

You head back the way you came... your steps feel lighter...
you get to the bright sunshine as you step out of the
forest and bask in the warmth of the sun.

Your heart is filled with gratitude as you walk across the meadow where you started your journey… feel the warmth of the sun on your skin.

If your eyes are closed… open them… notice your surroundings.

Notice your right hand, notice your left hand… notice your right foot, notice your left foot… notice your breathing.

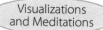

PRACTICE 10
IT IS WELL

Time: 3 minutes

Description: This breathing practice is about synchronizing your breath with a thought or an affirmation. When you breathe in, you think about inhaling things or characteristics you want more of, and when you breathe out, you exhale things you want less of. For example, I breathe in joy and breathe out stress. I breathe in kindness and breathe out sleeplessness. The items you name do not have to change with each breath. Repetition is good. Identifying and naming things you want more of or less of is a good skill to have and cultivates resilience. You can do this practice at the beginning or end of a session. It is also one you can do for yourself before your client arrives or between sessions on a busy day of appointments. Even doing the practice for a minute is a way to support your own well-being.

Script

Sitting in Chair Mountain... take a moment to sit and gather yourself... notice how you are breathing. How are you feeling?

This practice is like a prayer that is focused on, and coordinated with, your breathing. The idea is to think about what you want more of and what you want less of... on the inhale, silently say what you would like more of... and on the exhale, silently say what you want less of. Here's mine today: I breathe in more self-compassion... I exhale the desire to gossip.

Take a moment to think about what that might be for you today.

> *Allow about three to five seconds of silence.*

Open or close your eyes as you feel comfortable... let your breath be slow and even.

> *Demonstrate sitting in Chair Mountain and breathing at a slow, even pace.*

When you are ready... begin to inhale, and silently say a word that represents, or is, something you want more of... and exhale something you want less of... whatever is true for you today.

You can repeat the same words for the next minute or two, or come up with other words if you want... but don't try too hard... repetition is fine.

Bring your hand to your heart. If your eyes are closed,
open them… orient yourself to the space.

Notice how you are feeling right now. Has anything shifted?… maybe it
has… maybe it hasn't… but simply notice the moment as it is right now.

Let's complete this breath with a couple of sighing breaths… like this.

Inhale and exhale though the mouth… inhale and ha…
and again… inhale and ha.

Beautiful.

Epilogue

I have thought a lot about where and how yoga practices, such as the ones presented in this book, can be most effective. I realize that in the context in which I present them here, the practices represent interventions that can be utilized in certain circumstances or situations, like using the breath to mitigate feelings of anxiety. Certainly, I have observed, and the studies support, this downstream focus of yoga practice. However, it is also true that yoga shines its brightest when applied upstream—as a preventive measure—and when we remain curious, open-hearted, and open-handed with our practice. Upstream success is quiet and often hard to see, and it is even harder to quantify because it solves problems before they arise. However, as Dan Heath remarks in his new book, *Upstream*, it is these little changes that matter. These practices can bring about incremental changes that support the whole person and all the systems of the body, which is why I encourage daily practice. When you have performed your own experiments with these practices, I suggest that you recommend your clients consider integrating these practices into their daily routine as well.

If trauma is about rupture, then yoga is about connection, integration, and unity. It is about well-being and human flourishing. Although there are many documented physical benefits to practicing yoga, it is the *mental* health benefits that I am most passionate about. About a year ago, I realized that I had made this point strongly after my son, Lucca, asked if I would come and teach a weekly yoga class at his school during his final few months of high school. Such requests are rare and precious. Needless to say, I swiftly called teachers and administrators to clear the way. Because I was only teaching once a week for six weeks, I didn't have much time to make my points about yoga's mental health benefits, but as you will have noted from this book, giving someone the *experience* of a practice is much more powerful than simply describing and explaining it. Still, I wanted these precious but sleepy high schoolers to have knowledge *and* experience. I did my best to give them both.

About four weeks in, I did a review of what we had covered so far, leaning on a little Socratic inquiry to do so. "So what's the main reason we do yoga?" I asked. Surprisingly, some hands shot up (I wasn't even sure if they were all awake yet), and a tenth-grader blurted out, "So we don't kill ourselves!" I wasn't quite ready for the starkness of the comment, but it was spot on. I had repeatedly stated in class that practicing yoga was a way to care for ourselves and to gain self-awareness. We had talked about the awareness that yoga brings and the importance of noticing our feelings and asking for help, instead of waiting until a crisis occurs when the inevitable challenges of life feel overwhelming. When our six weeks together ended, even the initially reluctant students were sad to finish. The feedback I received overwhelmingly confirmed that the rest of their day went better when they started with yoga. This has been my experience also. And I hope it is (or soon will be) your experience too.

All good things come to an end at some point. So this is my attempt to bring something enormously unwieldly, yet deeply satisfying—this book—to a close. It has been rough writing my first book, but not to the point of saying *never again*. (Though a vacation now might be nice.) Here's a reality I would like you to know: I've had to lean into and practice every single practice in this book multiple times in order to manage my own mental and physical well-being during the process of writing it. I *had* to. And not just because I was writing about the practices, although that certainly was a factor. But because life is hard, beautiful, and messy. Life inevitably comes with its ups and downs. Having some of these practices as part of my daily routine helped me get out of bed in the mornings. So there's that.

Writing about any topic that has the word *trauma* in it day in and day out for many months is fraught with other people's suffering, not unsimilar to being a therapist. Like you, I have had to stand my ground and be consistent with my own self-care to make it through this season. I have wept buckets over some of the stories, case studies, and research I came across. I allowed myself to feel these things deeply in my body. As Dr. Albert Wong pointed out, "What we think and how we act matters. But it's not all that matters. How we feel in our bodies matters too. Or learning to feel in our bodies" (2020). My learning curve has been steep as I have come to terms with my own trauma, which is probably why I teach what I need to learn. I believe we all do to varying degrees. To that end, as we learn to feel with our bodies, we heal. I have healed. I *am* healing. I desire to be a regulating force in the world so people in my orbit can learn to do it for themselves. I am firmly anchoring myself in a ventral vagal state so I can meet you in sympathetic or dorsal. I believe that, together, we can get on the train to grand "ventral" station.

Finally, if you want the recipe for the secret sauce of the practices, it is love. The practices are done with love in mind. They are learned and shared with love in mind. What I mean by love was beautifully stated by Kate Bowler when she interviewed John Green about his book, *Turtles All the Way Down*:

> There's something John says at the end of the book, and I can tell you this much without spoiling it, and it was so smart that I wanted it as a tattoo. He writes, "Love is both how you become a person and why," and that sounded absolutely right to me. When we are defined by the things we didn't choose, by our bodies or our obstacles, or even our own pernicious thoughts, there is a way to feel like you are not eclipsed by these unwanted realities. Love, love that pours in from around us reminding us of who we are, and the act of loving, which shows us how to make our way forward, how to connect, how to dig deep into those soft places and pull out something that we can use as a gift. Love is both how and why. (2019)

This book is my love offering to help each of us find a way home to our bodies. Thank you for joining me on this journey. With grit and grace!

Summary of the Polyvagal Theory

Three Organizing Principles:

Hierarchical — Evolutionary/adaptive survival response	Neuroception — Constantly scanning for safety. Beneath conscious awareness.	Co-Regulation — Mutual regulation of physiological states between individuals	Nervous system activation	Possible health consequences
Ventral Vagal Myelinated, Parasympathetic • 200 million years ago • Newest — ● **GO**	• Safe • Rest/Digest • Tend/Befriend • Social Engagement System / *Feels happy* • Connected to world • Can reach out to others • Takes care of self • Feels regulated	In ventral vagal we: • Focus • Heal • Learn • Grow • Change / In safety we: • Care • Connect • Feel compassion • Are curious	Striated muscles of the face, heart, lungs	• Healthy heart • Regulated blood pressure • Healthy immune system • Good digestion • Quality sleep • Overall sense of well-being
Sympathetic • 400 million years ago • Newer — ● **PROCEED WITH CAUTION**	• Fight/Flight • Mobilize • Activate • Moving / *Feels anxious or angry* • Rush of adrenaline • Can't hear friendly voices • World feels dangerous, chaotic, unfriendly	In sympathetic we: • Run away • Defend • Energize / In safety we: • Play • Get things done • Engage in intimacy	Heart Lungs	• Increased blood pressure • Increased cholesterol • Vulnerability to illness • Sleep problems • Weight gain • Memory impairment • Headaches • Chronic neck/back pain • Stomach problems • Anxiety, panic attacks
Dorsal Vagal Unmyelinated, Parasympathetic • 500 million years ago • Oldest — ● **STOP**	• Life threat • Danger • Immobilize • Collapse • Feign death / *Feels alone, despair, nothingness* • Not feeling • Hopeless abandonment • Foggy • Too tired to think	In dorsal vagal we: • Faint • Defecate • Lose energy • Are paralyzed with fear • Dissociate / In safety we: • Meditate • Can be still • Savor • Relax	Gut	• Low blood pressure • Altered metabolism • Weight gain • Dissociation • Problems with memory • Depression • Chronic fatigue • Fibromyalgia • Stomach issues

Side labels:
- Rest/digest Tend/befriend
- Fight, fight or freeze
- Collapse

Bidirectional communication between the body (80%) and brain (20%)

This summary was created to be a visual and memory prompt of Polyvagal Theory and its implications. It is based on the work of Porges (2017) and Dana(2018).

Trauma-InformedYoga: Twelve Principles for Growth

These twelve principles for growth can be embodied most effectively in sequence. First are the inner resources of empowerment and worth. This is where we begin—from a place of "I can" and "I am worth the effort." Next come the physical basics: safety, breath, presence, and feeling. Then you are ready to self-regulate through authentic choice, grounding, ownership, and sustainability. Last, you enter the zone of what we call "mindful grit." Here you practice both self-compassion and self-determination.

Throughout your practice, you can work your way up and down this list. You can select one principle at a time or two that work together. For example, the physical basics can be paired with all the rest. As you practice the twelve principles, you will notice your connection with yourself, others, and the world shifting.

Principle for Growth	Yogis in Service: Trauma-Informed Yoga Recommendations
	Part 1: Inner Resources
Empowerment	• Emphasize the cognitive intention, "*I can.*" • Reinforce personal empowerment and effort over achievement and perfection. • Assist students and use props (e.g., yoga blocks, straps, and chairs) to help make poses and practices accessible to students. • Consider the yoga student as the expert in their own experience of yoga and growth (e.g., avoid telling students what poses, stress, challenges, or trauma should feel like or what recovery and growth should look like).
Worth	• Emphasize the cognitive intention, "*I am worth the effort.*" • Encourage commitment to presence and persistence in the face of challenges as an expression of self-worth. • Use the loving-kindness meditation (e.g., may you be happy, well, peaceful, and at ease; for self, beloved others, neutral others, difficult others, and world).

Part 2: Physical Basics	
Safety	• Emphasize the cognitive intention, *"I deserve to be safe."* • Prioritize physical and emotional safety in yoga practice. • Demonstrate trustworthiness through task clarity, consistency, and safe personal boundaries. • Avoid a perception of coercion. Teach by inviting students to try something as opposed to getting them to do something. • Consider mat placement (e.g., mats set up in a circle so there is no one behind anyone else, have options to place mats in the back row). • Cover exposed windows and mirrors for privacy. • Be predictable (e.g., tell the students what poses and challenges are coming, how long they will be holding poses, and follow a predictable class structure). • Use caution with yoga postures that may cause physical discomfort, be perceived as threatening, and trigger emotional reactions or flashbacks (e.g., poses that expose sensitive parts of the body, such as the groin area or chest). • When using physical assists, collaborate with individual students to determine their preferences. • Use verbal and visual assists by explaining or demonstrating the poses. • Consider using a nonverbal and private method for students to opt out of physical assists (e.g., asking them to raise their hand if they do not want assists or to place a chip on their mat). • Use caution with meditations, as some forms of meditation may trigger flashbacks. Collaborate with participants to create safe and supportive meditation practices. • Give permission for students to seek safety in class by adapting poses and practices (e.g., taking the final resting pose against the wall with their eyes open, or meditating with a softened gaze rather than closing their eyes). • Generally, use caution with women who are pregnant, individuals with disabilities, older adults, individuals with psychiatric illness, and individuals with severe trauma.
Breath	• Emphasize the cognitive intention, *"My breath is my most powerful tool."* • Frequently invite the participants to bring attention to their breath, the qualities of breath (e.g., pace, length, warmth, sound), the muscles that support breath, and the body movement associated with breath. • Offer choices rather than prescribing a way to breathe (e.g., add invitations to add deeper breath or to experiment with nasal breathing and to notice how that feels in the body). • Use meditations and relaxation sessions that focus on the breath, emphasizing breath awareness and the connection of the breath to heart rate and physical relaxation. • Note the associations between the breath and emotions, and provide opportunities for self-regulation (e.g., extended exhales for calming). • Use caution, as yogic breathing may be contraindicated for some individuals with psychosis. • Emphasize the cognitive intention, *"I work toward presence in my body."*

Presence	• Bring awareness to physical sensations as they are experienced in the body in the present moment (e.g., "You may notice the sensation of your feet pressing into your mat"). • Offer a safe and measured approach to interoceptive awareness by using tentative language (e.g., inviting participants to pay attention, suggesting they may notice a feeling or sensation when they move their bodies in a certain way, recognizing that they may also not notice or feel anything). • Use suggestive language to emphasize that participants are not required to move in such a way or to feel a particular feeling. • Encourage students to notice the experience they are having in their bodies and then highlight the value in not turning the experience into a story or an emotion. • Consider that being in the present moment and being aware of body sensations can feel uncomfortable, even terrifying, to some trauma survivors. • Utilize meditation and relaxation practices that encourage physical presence (e.g., body scan technique and systematic relaxation). • Help bring awareness to the body through verbal cues and physical assists (with permission).
Feeling	• Emphasize the cognitive intention, "*I feel so I can heal*." • Remind students that feelings in the body can take on many forms, including not feeling anything (e.g., feeling numb) or feeling big feelings. • Bring attention to the wave (e.g., arising and passing) of physical sensations and feeling states. • Remind students that sometimes simply noticing and allowing emotions is enough. • Encourage students to use breath, grounding, and positive self-talk—"I am worth the effort" and "I feel so I can heal"—as they observe the wave of emotions rising and passing during their practice. • Teach the "Soften, Soothe, Allow" meditation by Kristen Neff.
	**Part 3: Self-Regulation**
Grounding	• Emphasize the cognitive intention, "*My body is a source for connection, coping, and guidance*." • Encourage students to consider that connecting with the body is a resource for connecting with themselves and others, as well as for coping and guidance. • Remind students that, at any given moment, they can connect to their physical sensations as a means of grounding themselves from emotional or physical arousal, and they can breathe intentionally to calm themselves. • Prompt students to check into their bodies as a source of information to help them make choices in the present moment (e.g., "Notice the sensations in your upper leg. You may want to deepen the pose or ease out of the pose"). • Within the context of communication, choice, and permission, consider that physical assists may have therapeutic value in helping some yoga students tolerate safe, nurturing, and positive touch from another. • Emphasize the cognitive intention, "*I can find choice in the present moment*."

Choice	• Create an atmosphere of ongoing, informed consent. To do this, be clear about what you are requesting of the students, offer a menu of options, and always include the ability to adapt a posture and to opt out. • Invite participants to make a connection between the feeling in their bodies and the choices they are making. • Frequently phrase guidance as suggestions and invitations rather than commands (e.g., "Consider..", "If you'd like…", "You can choose…", or "One option is…"). • Teach the class at a pace that allows yoga students to make a choice. If the pace is too fast, it may feel like there is no choice. • Reinforce the contention that there is no right or wrong choice regarding what feels right for them in this moment.
Ownership	• Emphasize the cognitive intention, "*I can create the conditions for safety and growth.*" • Prompt students to use the physical sensations coming from their bodies to make safe and effective choices in poses and actions. • Encourage students to take ownership of their yoga practice by listening to teacher cues and prompts in equal measure to their own internal cues and prompts. • Support student ownership through your own practice of acceptance and allowing in the yoga room.
Sustainability	• Emphasize the cognitive intention, "*I can create a balance between structure and change.*" • Encourage a balance of effort and rest through instruction. • Work to create a yoga space that honors and celebrates a safe and sustainable practice, as well as progress in practice. • Reinforce the contention that yoga is a mindfulness-based practice that may not be a linear path toward more advanced poses and practices but, rather, a deepening of awareness, presence, and connection.
Part 4: Mindful Grit	
Compassion	• Emphasize the cognitive intention, "*I honor the individual path of recovery and growth.*" • Consider that resistance can be associated with fear and anxiety and can be addressed with support and compassion. • Remind students that growth is a process of gains and setbacks. • Remind students that the moment we begin to judge, we lose connection to presence in the moment. • Provide an inclusive yoga space with props (e.g., chairs, straps, and blocks), as well as acceptance of a wide range of experiences within the yoga space.
Self-Determination	• Emphasize the cognitive intention, "*I work toward the possibility of effectiveness and growth in my own life.*" • In poses and practices, ask student to notice what is effective for them. • Remind students of the uniqueness of each path. There is no right path for all. • Teach from a sense of possibility for all of your students. • Remind yourself and your students that stress and trauma need not determine the outcomes of one's life.

Used with permission of Cook-Cottone et al. (2017)

Noticing Logs

Our bodies are giving us information all of the time. However, we may not notice because of the cluttered thoughts and level of distraction we experience. When we set aside time and set an intention to actively listen to what the body is saying, we get better at gathering information. The following two noticing logs are intended for you to record the sensations or feelings you experience during your day *as you notice them*, as well as any notes about the experience. As you practice noticing and recording these things in the moment, it will help you notice them more. More noticing will lead to increased self-awareness, and more awareness will help you to better regulate your nervous system.

The first noticing log is more freeform in nature, whereas the second log is more visual and explicitly guides your observations to certain body parts. You can use one or both logs, whichever appeals to you the most. Begin by using the log on a weekly basis, and work your way up to completing it daily until it becomes second nature to notice what is going on in your body. When you reach this point, it will become easier to choose and apply a practice that you have learned in therapy.

Noticing Log #1

Begin by just noticing what is going on in your body right now. No need to change or judge anything you are doing, just notice your body in this moment. Is there a pattern emerging over time?

Date and Time of Day	Body Part	Sensations	Feelings	Observations

Noticing Log #2

Begin by just noticing what is going on in your body right now. No need to change or judge anything you are doing, just notice your body in this moment. Is there a pattern emerging over time?

Date and Time of Day	Body Part	Sensations or Feelings	Observations
			(e.g., I think as soon as I am awake.)
			(e.g., I brush my teeth before I start my day.)
			(e.g., I drink water upon arising. I notice I am not hungry.)
			(e.g., I listen for the sounds of the day… people in the house, traffic, weather.)
			(e.g., My eyes notice the light.)
			(e.g., My eyelashes flicker to soften the light.)
			(e.g., My feet get a nice ankle rotation before I get up. They feel cold from the air conditioning.)

			(e.g., I move my lips into funny shapes because it is supposed to promote youthful looks. I smile.)
			(e.g., I sniff the air. Is it hot or cold?)
			(e.g., My hands reach for my phone to see what time it is.)
			(e.g., My fingertips feel the softness of the curtains as I open them.
			(e.g., I am aware that my heart is beating. It speeds up as my thoughts speed up.)
			(e.g., My lungs feel sluggish. My breathing feels shallow and slow.)
			(e.g., My arm muscles feel strong when I do a Downward Dog.)
			(e.g., I am not really aware of my kidneys. But I am grateful I have them.)
			(e.g., My body in its entirety feels pain free, slow, and sluggish as I emerge from sleep.)

How I Support My Body Checklist

This checklist is a reminder that you do indeed have a body that needs your attention throughout the day. As you go through each day, keep this checklist handy and take some time to record how your body is feeling and what your mood is like as you complete these activities (don't worry if you don't complete everything). As you make note of these seemingly obvious bodily needs and functions, you may start reconnecting with your body in a kind and thoughtful way. Noticing and attending to these needs as they arise can cultivate a nurturing and honoring relationship with your body. The checklist is also a reminder of all of the activities that contribute to self-care.

Activity	Time of Day	Body Sensations	Emotions
Hydrate			
Go to the bathroom			
Brush teeth			
Wash face			
Move my body			
Shower			
Bathe			
Dress			
Make breakfast			
Do dishes			
Listen to something inspirational			
Read something inspirational			
Make a warm drink			
Review my daily schedule			
Gather things to leave the house for work			
Gather things to work at home			
Go to the bathroom			

Begin work			
Lunch			
More bathroom breaks			
Hydrate			
Leave to come home from work			
Run errands			
Make dinner			
Clean up			
Do chores			
Take time for hobbies			
Recover from my day			
Put my feet up			
Do a social media check-in			
Walk/exercise			
Go to the gym			
Read			
Go out			
Get ready for bed			
Communicate with people who matter to me			
Take a shower			
Have physical intimacy			
Practice my bedtime ritual			
Go to sleep			

Therapist Worksheet

This worksheet will help you track the practices that you introduce to your client. By keeping track of what you have tried, what worked, why it worked, how you felt about using it, and how your client felt about using it, you will increase your confidence and knowledge as to how to best use the practices. This worksheet will also help you keep track of and organize your own observations and inquiries.

Date	Practice	What worked?	Why?	What did you notice in your client?	What did you notice in you?	Observations

Administering the ACEs Questionnaire: Therapist Instructions

The following ACEs Questionnaire is a validated screening tool for trauma that you can use during your intake process if you don't already have one. Completing the test for yourself first is useful information for your own journey and is perhaps a reason to seek therapy for yourself. The questionnaire may point to most, if not all, of the reasons your client is seeking counseling. Maintaining an awareness of the dose-response relationship is a key to informing your treatment plan, meaning that as the number of ACEs increases, psychological health decreases.

You can verbally administer the questionnaire to clients in person if the context allows for confidentiality and safety. However, it is equally valid to allow clients to complete the questionnaire on paper with the understanding that they can decline either option. Keep in mind that this questionnaire is not comprehensive in nature and is only a screening tool to point to the need for more in-depth assessment and inquiry.

When administering the questionnaire, Patrick Tennant gives clinicians a timely reminder: "It is critical that clinicians be aware of co-morbidities associated with the ACEs (especially the increased risk of suicidality and self-harm) and of the requirements of their mandated reporting status that may arise from assessing trauma history" (n.d.). For this reason, he emphasizes that clinicians use grounding techniques after screening clients to make sure they feel safe and regulated before leaving the session. Some therapists have argued about the ethics of bringing up past abuse. However, co-investigator of the ACEs Study, Vince Felitti, found that asking people about the worst things they have ever experienced left them feeling understood and accepted (Felitti and Anda, 2007). Edwards et al. (2007) came to the conclusion that indeed it is ethical to ask about adverse childhood experiences, otherwise an important predictor of problems in life may be overlooked.

ACEs Questionnaire: What Is Your ACE Score?

To determine your ACE score, answer yes or no to the following ten questions. The number of "yes" answers gives you your score. Finding out your score is a good step to confirming some knowledge about yourself. It is simply a starting point.

Prior to your 18th birthday:

1. Did a parent or other adult in the household often or very often… swear at you, insult you, put you down, or humiliate you? Or act in a way that made you afraid that you might be physically hurt?

    No_____   Yes_____

2. Did a parent or other adult in the household often or very often… push, grab, slap, or throw something at you? Or ever hit you so hard that you had marks or were injured?

    No_____   Yes_____

3. Did an adult or person at least five years older than you ever… touch or fondle you or have you touch their body in a sexual way? Or attempt or actually have oral, anal, or vaginal intercourse with you?

    No_____   Yes_____

4. Did you often or very often feel that… no one in your family loved you or thought you were important or special? Or your family didn't look out for each other, feel close to each other, or support each other?

    No_____   Yes_____

5. Did you often or very often feel that … you didn't have enough to eat, had to wear dirty clothes, and had no one to protect you? Or your parents were too drunk or high to take care of you or take you to the doctor if you needed it?

    No_____   Yes_____

6. Were your parents ever separated or divorced?

    No_____   Yes_____

7. Was your mother or stepmother… often or very often pushed, grabbed, slapped, or had something thrown at her? Or was she sometimes, often, or very often kicked, bitten, hit with a fist, or hit with something hard? Or was she ever repeatedly hit for at least a few minutes or threatened with a gun or knife?

    No_____   Yes_____

8. Did you live with anyone who was a problem drinker or alcoholic, or who used street drugs?

    No_____   Yes_____

9. Was a household member depressed or mentally ill, or did a household member attempt suicide?

    No_____   Yes_____

10. Did a household member go to prison?

    No_____   Yes_____

Now add up your "Yes" answers. This is your ACE Score: _____

Now that you have your ACE score, you can go to the following website to find out what it means at the acestoohigh.com/got-your-ace-score/.

Reprinted with permission from https://acestoohigh.com/got-your-ace-score/

Resources

Over the years, I have found particular books, music, podcasts, and so forth that have added to my knowledge base in many ways. The list here represents a generous sampling of what have been important resources on my learning journey.

RECOMMENDED READINGS

Brown, B. (2018). *Dare to lead: Brave work. Tough conversations. Whole hearts.* New York: Random House.

Bondy, D. (2019). *Yoga for everyone: 50 poses for every type of body.* Indianapolis: D. K. Publishing.

Channing Brown, A. (2018). *I'm still here: Black dignity in a world made for whiteness.* Colorado Springs: Convergent Books.

Cohen Harper, J. & Breen-Gonzalez, M. (2019). *Mindful chair yoga card deck.* Eau Claire: PESI.

Cook-Cottone, C. (2015). *Mindfulness and yoga for self-regulation: A primer for mental health professionals.* New York: Springer.

Dana, D. (2018). *The polyvagal theory in therapy: Engaging the rhythm of regulation.* New York: W.W. Norton.

Desikachar, T. K. V. (1995). *The heart of yoga: Developing a personal practice.* Rochester, VT: Inner Traditions.

Emerson, D., & Hopper, E. (2011). *Overcoming trauma through yoga: Reclaiming the body.* Berkeley: North Atlantic Books.

Forbes, B. (2011). *Yoga for emotional balance: Simple practices to help relieve anxiety and depression.* Boston: Shambhala.

Goldberg, E. (2016). *The path of modern yoga: The history of an embodied spiritual practice.* Rochester, VT: Inner Traditions.

Guo, W. & Vulchi, P. (2019). *Tell me who you are: Sharing our stories of race, culture, and identity.* New York: Tarcher Perigee.

Hari, J. (2018). *Lost connections: Uncovering the real causes of depression—and the unexpected solutions.* New York: Bloomsbury Publishing.

Kendi, I. (2019). *How to be an anti-racist.* New York: One World.

Kress, R. (2020). *Awakening your inner radiance with LifeForce Yoga: Strategies for coping with depression, anxiety, and trauma.* Lebanon, OR: LifeForce Yoga.

Levine, P. (1997). *Waking the tiger: Healing trauma.* Berkeley: North Atlantic Books.

Loehr, J., & Migdow, J. (1999). *Breathe in, breathe out: Inhale energy and exhale stress by guiding and controlling your breathing.* New York: Time-Life.

McGonigal, K. (2009). *Yoga for pain relief: Simple practices to calm your mind and heal your chronic pain.* Oakland, CA: New Harbinger Publications.

Parker, G. (2020). *Restorative yoga for ethnic and race-based stress and trauma.* London: Singing Dragon.

Porges, S. W. (2017). *The pocket guide to the polyvagal theory: The transformative power of feeling safe.* New York: W. W. Norton.

Steele, C. (2011). *Whistling Vivaldi: How stereotypes affect us and what we can do.* New York: W.W. Norton.

Stevens, J. (2012, October 8). The Adverse Childhood Experiences Study—the largest public health study you never heard of. *Huffington Post.* Retrieved from https://www.huffpost.com/entry/the-adverse-childhood-exp_1_b_1943647

Thompson, C. (2010). *The anatomy of the soul: Surprising connections between neuroscience and spiritual practices that can transform your life and relationships.* Chicago: Tyndale House.

van der Kolk, B. (2014). *The body keeps the score: Brain, mind, and body in the healing of trauma.* New York: Penguin Books.

Walker, M. P. (2017). *Why we sleep: Unlocking the power of sleep and dreams.* New York: Scribner.

Weintraub, A. (2012). *Yoga skills for therapists: Effective practices for mood management.* New York: W. W. Norton.

CDS

Atmospheres: Dolphin Dance by Jeff Wolpert

Chakra Suite by Steven Halpern

Comfort Zone by Steven Halpern

Dancing at the Gate by Dana Cunningham

Healing Touch I by Nadama

Healing Touch II by Nadama

Heart to Heart by Nadama

Meditation to Beat the Blues by Amy Weintraub

The Sacred Well by 2002

DVDS

Absolute Beginner Yoga DVD with Joanne Spence

Get Fit Where You Sit Chair Yoga with Lakshmi Voelker

Just My Size DVD with Megan Garcia

LifeForce Yoga Level I with Amy Weintraub

Lilias! Complete Yoga Fitness for Beginners with Lilias Folan

Viniyoga Therapy for Depression with Gary Kraftsow

Viniyoga Therapy for Anxiety with Gary Kraftsow

Yoga for Stress Reduction with Hala Khouri

Yoga Thrive with Susi Hately

Yoga Tune Up˚ Quick Fix Rx with Jill Miller

FREE APPS

Centering Prayer: A method of silent, breath-focused prayer.

EQ Coach: Learn how to be more emotionally intelligent with this skill-building app.

Happify: Build skills for lasting happiness and a more fulfilling life.

MindShift: A pocket-size toolbox of coping skills to go.

Saagara: Provides a helpful visual and audio support for a breathing practice.

Stop, Breathe & Think: Allows you to practice mindfulness and meditation anytime, anywhere.

SuperBetter: A game that helps build personal resilience.

10% Happier: Guided meditations, videos, talks, and sleep content will help you build your meditation practice and stick with it.

PODCASTS

Everything Happens with Kate Bowler

Good Ancestor with Layla F. Saad

Life as Spiritual Practice with Lauren Burdette

Move Your DNA with Katy Bowman

On Being with Krista Tippett

Polyvagal Podcast with Justin Sunseri

Restoring the Soul with Michael John Cusick
The Tim Ferriss Show with Tim Ferriss
The Trauma Therapist with Guy MacPherson
Unlocking Us with Brené Brown

YOGA TRAININGS

LifeForce Yoga: An evidence-based mood regulation protocol that supports those with anxiety, depression, and PTSD using accessible yoga tools (www.yogafordepression.com)

Subtle Yoga: Provides holistic education and training for yoga professionals and health care providers (www.subtleyoga.com)

Functional Synergy: Trains yoga teachers how to have functional, pain-free movement with yoga therapy (www.functionalsynergy.com)

Yoga Roots on Location: Trains yoga teachers and leads embodied antiracist organizing through Raja yoga (www.yogarootsonlocation.com)

Yoga Tune-Up: Uses a fitness therapy format designed to eradicate pain, improve posture, and enhance performance through a unique blend of corrective exercises, self-message, and yoga (www.tuneupfitness.com)

Yogafit: Emphasizes sports science and alignment principles, as well as the ancient traditions of yoga (www.yogafit.com)

WEBSITES

ACES Connection: A human and digital catalyst that unites people, organizations, systems, and communities in the worldwide ACEs movement (www.acesconnection.com)

ACES Too High: Reports on research about adverse childhood experiences, including developments in epidemiology, neurobiology, and the biomedical and epigenetic consequences of toxic stress (www.acestoohigh.com)

ADHD & Marriage: Helps adults thrive in relationships impacted by ADHD (www.adhdmarriage.com)

HeartMath: Helps people experience science-based technology and programs for taking charge of your life (www.heartmath.com)

Kira Willey: Provides music, movement, and mindfulness for kids (www.kirawilley.com)

LifeSpa: Provides alternative health and wellness information with a specialty in Ayurveda with Dr. John Douillard (www.lifespa.com)

Remember to Breathe: Teaches simple techniques that balance your brain and positively affect everything in your life (www.remember-to-breathe.org)

Slow-Movement Maven: Provides information on how to heal physically and mentally with gentle yoga and breathing exercises (www.joannespence.com)

Yoga in Schools: Empowers students and teachers with yoga-inspired exercises to promote lifetime wellness, with the goal of making yoga available in all schools (www.yogainschools.org)

Yogis in Service: Creates access to connection—to self, others, and the community—through yoga practice and the stress management tools of yoga (www.yogisinservice.org)

RETREAT CENTERS

It can be helpful to schedule regular time away for rest and renewal or professional development. Each of the retreat centers here offers space for both. Advance planning is necessary to reserve your spot. Schedules are usually available six months in advance. There are many retreat centers around the country and world, but these are just a handful I have personally enjoyed or taught at.

Kripalu Yoga and Retreat Center (Lenox, MA)

Omega Institute (Rhinebeck, NY)

Villa Maria Education and Spirituality Center (Villa Maria, PA)

Graymoor Spiritual Life Center (Garrison, NY)

Garrison Institute (Garrison, NY)

Jesuit Retreat Center (Parma, OH)

Martina Renewal Center (Pittsburgh, PA)

YOGA ORGANIZATIONS

International Association of Yoga Therapy: Supports research and education in yoga and serves as a professional organization for yoga teachers and yoga therapists worldwide (www.iayt.org)

The Minded Institute: Provides scientifically informed long and short trainings for yoga and health professionals in yoga therapy for mental health and beyond (www.themindedinstitute.com)

Yoga Alliance: A national voluntary registry of yoga teachers that fosters and supports high-quality, safe, accessible, and equitable teaching of yoga (www.yogaalliance.org)

Yoga Service Council: Maximizes the effectiveness, sustainability, and impact of those working to make yoga and mindfulness equally accessible to all (www.yogaservicecouncil.org)

Christians Practicing Yoga: Studies the intersections of yoga philosophy and Christian theology—and the practices of both—in order to provide support, education, and community for an interdenominational Christian audience (www. christianspracticingyoga.com)

References

For your convenience, sample forms are available
for download at www.pesi.com/traumayoga

American Psychological Association. (2020). *Trauma*. Retrieved from https://www.apa.org/topics/trauma/

Bowler, K. (2019). *Chronic not curable: An interview with author, John Greene* [Audio podcast]. Retrieved from https://katebowler.com/podcasts/john-green-chronic-not-curable/

Brand, P., & Yancey, P. (1997). *The gift of pain: Why we hurt and what we can do about it.* Grand Rapids, MI: Zondervan.

Breus, M. (2020, February 29). *5 surprising health problems tied to poor sleep* [Blog post]. Retrieved from https://thesleepdoctor.com/2020/02/29/5-surprising-health-problems-tied-to-poor-sleep/

Brown, B. (2018). *Dare to lead: Brave work. Tough conversations. Whole hearts.* New York: Random House.

Brown, J. (2013). *Gentle is the new advanced* [Blog post]. Retrieved from https://www.jbrownyoga.com/blog/2013/08/gentle-is-the-new-advanced#commenting

Centers for Disease Control. (2018). *6 guiding principles to a trauma-informed approach.* Retrieved from https://www.cdc.gov/cpr/infographics/6_principles_trauma_info.htm

Cook-Cottone, C. (2013). Dosage as a critical variable in yoga therapy research. *International Journal of Yoga Therapy, 23*(2), 11–12.

Cook-Cottone, C. (2015). *Mindfulness and yoga for self-regulation: A primer for mental health professionals.* New York: Springer.

Cook-Cottone, C., Vigne, M. L., Guyker, W., Travers, L., & Lemish, E. (2017). Trauma-informed yoga: An embodied, cognitive-relational framework. *International Journal of Complementary & Alternative Medicine, 9*(1), 1–10. https://doi.org/10.15406/ijcam.2017.09.00284

Dana, D. (2018). *The polyvagal theory in therapy: Engaging the rhythm of regulation.* New York: W. W. Norton.

Elliott, S. B. (2005). *The new science of breath: Coherent breathing for autonomic nervous system balance, health and well-being.* Allen, TX: Coherence Press.

Emerson, D., & Hopper, E. (2011). *Overcoming trauma through yoga: Reclaiming the body.* Berkeley: North Atlantic Books.

Felitti, V. J. (2002). The relation between adverse childhood experiences and adult health: Turning gold into lead. *The Permanente Journal, 6*(1), 44–47.

Felitti, V. J., Anda, R. F., Nordenberg, D., Williamson, D. F., Spitz, A. M., Edwards, V., Koss, M. P., & Marks, J. S. (1998). Relationship of childhood abuse and household dysfunction to many of the leading causes of death in adults: The Adverse Childhood Experiences (ACE) Study. *American Journal of Preventive Medicine, 14*(4), 245–258. https://doi.org/10.1016/S0749-3797(98)00017-8

Godman, H. (2016, September). *How much water should I drink?* Harvard Health Publishing: Harvard Medical School. Retrieved from https://www.health.harvard.edu/staying-healthy/how-much-water-should-you-drink

Hannaford, C. (1995). *Smart moves: Why learning is not all in your head.* Salt Lake City: Great River Books.

Hately, S. (2010, September). *Therapeutic yoga intensive.* Functional Synergy Yoga Teacher Training, Toronto, ON, Canada.

Heath, D. (2020). *Upstream: The quest to solve problems before they happen.* New York: Simon & Schuster.

Hodas, G. (2006). *Responding to childhood trauma: The promise and practice of trauma informed care.* Harrisburg, PA: Pennsylvania Office of Mental Health and Substance Abuse Services. Retrieved from http://www.childrescuebill.org/VictimsOfAbuse/RespondingHodas.pdf

Huckshorn, K. (2004, October). *Creating recovery facilitating systems of care.* Symposium conducted at the 2004 Best Practices Symposium: Transforming Knowledge and Research into Practice in the Public Mental Health Sector, Savannah, GA. Retrieved from https://www.nasmhpd.org/sites/default/files//mdsymp_proceedings_2004.pdf

Illinois State Board of Education. (n.d.). *Illinois standards in social and emotional learning*. Retrieved from https://www.isbe.net/Documents/SEL_goal1.pdf

International Association of Yoga Therapists. (n.d.). *Contemporary definitions of yoga therapy*. Retrieved from https://www.iayt.org/page/ContemporaryDefiniti

Jennings, A. (2007). *The story of a child's path to mental illness and suicide*. Retrieved from: http://www.theannainstitute.org/presentations.html

Kabat-Zinn, J. (1994). *Wherever you go, there you are*. New York: Hachette Books.

Kilpatrick, D. G., Resnick, H. S., Milanak, M. E., Miller, M. W., Keyes, K. M., & Friedman, M. J. (2013). National estimates of exposure to traumatic events and PTSD prevalence using DSM-IV and DSM-5 criteria. *Journal of Traumatic Stress, 26*(5), 537–547.

Khouri, H. (2019). *Yoga for self-regulation and trauma* [Audio course]. Off the Mat, Into the World. Retrieved from https://otmtraining.offthematintotheworld.org/p/yoga-for-self-regulation-and-trauma-course-recording-2019

Kolber, A. (2020). *Trying softer: A fresh approach to move us out of anxiety, stress, and survival mode—and into a life of connection and joy*. Carol Stream, IL: Tyndale Momentum.

Kress, R. (2019). *LifeForce Yoga practitioner training for mental health: Level 2 manual*. Lebanon, OR: LifeForce Yoga.

Kress, R. (2020). *Awakening your inner radiance with LifeForce Yoga: Strategies for coping with depression, anxiety & trauma*. Tucson, AZ: LifeForce Yoga.

Loehr, J., & Migdow, J. (1999). *Breathe in, breathe out: Inhale energy and exhale stress by guiding and controlling your breathing*. New York: Time-Life.

McCall, T. (2007). *Yoga as medicine: The yogic prescription for health and healing*. New York: Bantam Dell.

McKeown, P. (2015). *The oxygen advantage: Simple, scientifically proven breathing techniques*. New York: Harper Collins.

Moseley, L. (2011, November 11). *Why things hurt* [Video file]. Retrieved from https://youtu.be/gwd-wLdIHjs

Mulder, T., Zijlstra, S., Zijlstra, W., & Hochstenbach, J. (2004). The role of motor imagery in learning a totally novel movement. *Experimental Brain Research, 154*(2), 211–217. https://doi.org/10.1007/s00221-003-1647-6

Payne, P., Levine, P., & Crane-Godreau, M. (2015). Somatic experiencing: Using interoception and proprioception as core elements of trauma therapy. *Frontiers in Psychology, 6*(93), 1–18. https://doi.org/10.3389/fpsyg.2015.00093

Porges, S. W. (2017). *The pocket guide to the polyvagal theory: The transformative power of feeling safe*. New York: W. W. Norton.

Prather, A. A., Janicki-Deverts, D., Hall, M. H., & Cohen, S. (2015). Behaviorally assessed sleep and susceptibility to the common cold. *Sleep, 38*(9), 1353–1359.

Reuben, A. (2015, December 14). When PTSD is contagious. *The Atlantic*. Retrieved from: https://www.theatlantic.com/health/archive/2015/12/ptsd-secondary-trauma/420282/

Ross, A., Friedmann, E., Bevans, M., & Thomas, S. (2012). Frequency of yoga practice predicts health: Results from a national survey of yoga practice. *Evidence-Based Complementary and Alternative Medicine, 2012*, Article ID 983258.

Satchidananda, S. (1985). *The yoga sutras of Patanjali. Pocket edition*. Buckingham, VA: Integral Publications.

Singleton, M. (2010). *Yoga body: The origins of modern postural practice*. Oxford, UK: Oxford University Press.

Singleton, M. (2011, February 4). The ancient & modern roots of yoga. *Yoga Journal*. Retrieved from https://www.yogajournal.com/yoga-101/yoga-s-greater-truth

Stiles, M. (2002). *Yoga Therapy Center: Joint freeing series. Pavanmuktasana* [Handout]. Holyoke, MA: Author.

Streeter, C. C., Gerbarg, P. L., Nielsen, G. H., Brown, R. P., Jensen, J. E., & Silveri, M. M. (2018). Effects of yoga on thalamic gamma-aminobutyric acid, mood and depression: Analysis of two randomized controlled trials. *Neuropsychiatry, 8*(6), 1923–1939.

Strom, M. (2017, April 15). *IA-30: Max Strom's 30 minutes inner axis practice* [Video file]. Retrieved from https://www.youtube.com/watch?v=RlB6rH8bcVk

Substance Abuse and Mental Health Services Administration. (2014, July). *SAMHSA's Concept of Trauma and Guidance for a Trauma-Informed Approach*. HHS Publication No. (SMA) 14-4884. Rockville, MD: Substance Abuse and Mental Health Services Administration. Retrieved from https://store.samhsa.gov/system/files/sma14-4884.pdf

Tan, S-Y. (2000). *Rest: Experiencing God's peace in a restless world*. Ann Arbor, MI: Vine Books.

Tennant, C. (n.d.). *How to administer a trauma screening using the ACEs Questionnaire*. The University of Texas at Austin: Texas Institute for Child & Family Wellbeing. Retrieved from https://txicfw.socialwork.utexas.edu/trauma-screening-aces-questionnaire/

van der Kolk, B. (2014). *The body keeps the score: Brain, mind, and body in the healing of trauma*. New York: Penguin Books.

Vesalius, A. (1543). *De humani corporis fabrica libri septem*. Padua, Italy: Padua School of Medicine.

Walker, M. P. (2017). *Why we sleep: Unlocking the power of sleep and dreams*. New York: Scribner.

Weber, K. (2019, October 23). *Teaching yoga and making money—Can we talk?* [Blog post]. Retrieved from https://subtleyoga.com/teaching-yoga-and-making-money-can-we-talk/

Weintraub, A. (2012). *Yoga skills for therapists: Effective practices for mood management*. New York: W. W. Norton.

Wong, A. (2020). *You can't think your way out of trauma: The importance of the body in psychotherapy*. Symposium presented at the 2020 Embodied Trauma Conference (Online).

Yoga Journal and Yoga Alliance. (2016). Yoga in America Study. *Yoga Journal*. Retrieved from https://www.yogajournal.com/page/yogainamericastudy

Made in United States
Troutdale, OR
06/24/2023

10773676R00120